PIA ARKE

Pia Arke

Edited by Lærke Rydal Jørgensen and Anders Kold
Graphic Design: Marie d'Origny Lübecker
Photo Editor: Sidse Buck and Kim Hansen
Editorial Assistant: Pernille G. Johansson
Proofreading: James Manley

Cover, front: Detail of *Self-Portrait*, 1992
Black-and-white photograph, 30 × 25 cm
Private collection
Photo: Peter Baastrup
Cover, back: Photo of Pia Arke's pinhole camera in Narsaq
Photo: Scan from negative from Pia Arke Estate
Spine: Detail of *Legend III*, 1999
Collage: paper, pencil, pen, gelatin silver print, wood and sugar, 197 × 165 cm
Louisiana Museum of Modern Art
Acquired with funding from Anker Fonden
Photo: Poul Buchard / Brøndum & Co.

Litho/Print: Narayana Press
ISBN: 978-87-93659-43-8
Printed in Denmark 2021
www.louisiana.dk

Content

Foreword

Pia Arke (1958-2007) is one of a kind in the history of recent Danish art. Her themes involve identity, belonging, the meaning of places, and the relationship between her two home countries, Greenland and Denmark. Arke's art practice was nomadic: In the late 1980s, while at the Royal Danish Academy of Fine Arts, she started taking self-portraits in her Copenhagen apartment. A few years later, she brought her homemade, person-sized pinhole camera to Greenland, photographing the landscape of her childhood. Back in Copenhagen, she photographed her nude body on the backdrop of these landscape images.

Above all a photographer, Arke also worked in painting, collage, video and performance. A key device for Arke was to mix other people's images with her own. Combing through archives, she found photos of Greenlandic women, taken by the explorer Robert E. Peary in the late 19th century, and photos of her own mother, taken by Sven Lund Jensen, a Danish telegraph operator, in the mid-20th century. Maps of Greenland are another motif. Arke's last major project, the book *Stories from Scoresbysund*, is a collage of pictures and stories from the land of her birth, viewed through the prism of Greenland's colonial history. In this way, Arke returned people to places that once were theirs. This aspect of her work can be defined as artistic research – critically and often humorously, Arke examined subjects like mapmaking, history writing and science.

Pia Arke's art builds on the work of notable women artists from the 1960s on who experimented with their identity in front of the camera, allowing the image to contribute and guide them. This tradition is represented in the Louisiana's collection by the work of artists like Cindy Sherman, Ana Mendieta, Birgit Jürgensen and Francesca Woodman.

A few years before Arke's untimely death in 2007, the artist collective Kuratorisk Aktion did important work to ensure that Arke's art would not be forgotten. In 2010, they organized the first retrospective of the artist's work, *Tupilakosaurus*, at Den Frie Centre of Contemporary Art in Copenhagen. The Louisiana's exhibition would hardly have been possible without their efforts. In recent years, the museum has acquired 15 works by Arke for its collection. The *Pia Arke* exhibition has been a long time in the making. Meanwhile, international interest in the artist's work and history has grown. International museums have started collecting her work, which was also included in the 2018 Istanbul Biennial and will be shown later this year at the São Paulo Biennial. Moreover, the Louisiana's exhibition will be on view in Denmark until the end of 2022, travelling first to Kunsten Museum of Modern Art in Aalborg and then to Kunstmuseum Brandts in Odense.

In this catalogue, a number of contributors shine new light on Arke's work from different angles – science, art, cultural criticism and literature. We thank Darren Almond, Erik Gant, Helle Fagralid, Stefan Jonsson, Jessie Kleemann, Kim Leine, Minik Rosing, Laura Smith and Erik Steffensen for their contributions.

Over the course of this project, the Louisiana has worked closely with the artist's son, Søren Arke, and his father, Michael Petersen. We owe them a great debt of gratitude. We are deeply thankful to the New Carlsberg Foundation for supporting the publication of this catalogue. Special thanks to the C.L. David Foundation and Collection, supporter of the exhibition series *Louisiana On Paper*, of which the Pia Arke exhibition is part. Finally, we thank our colleagues at Kunsten and Kunstmuseum Brandts.

Poul Erik Tøjner
Director

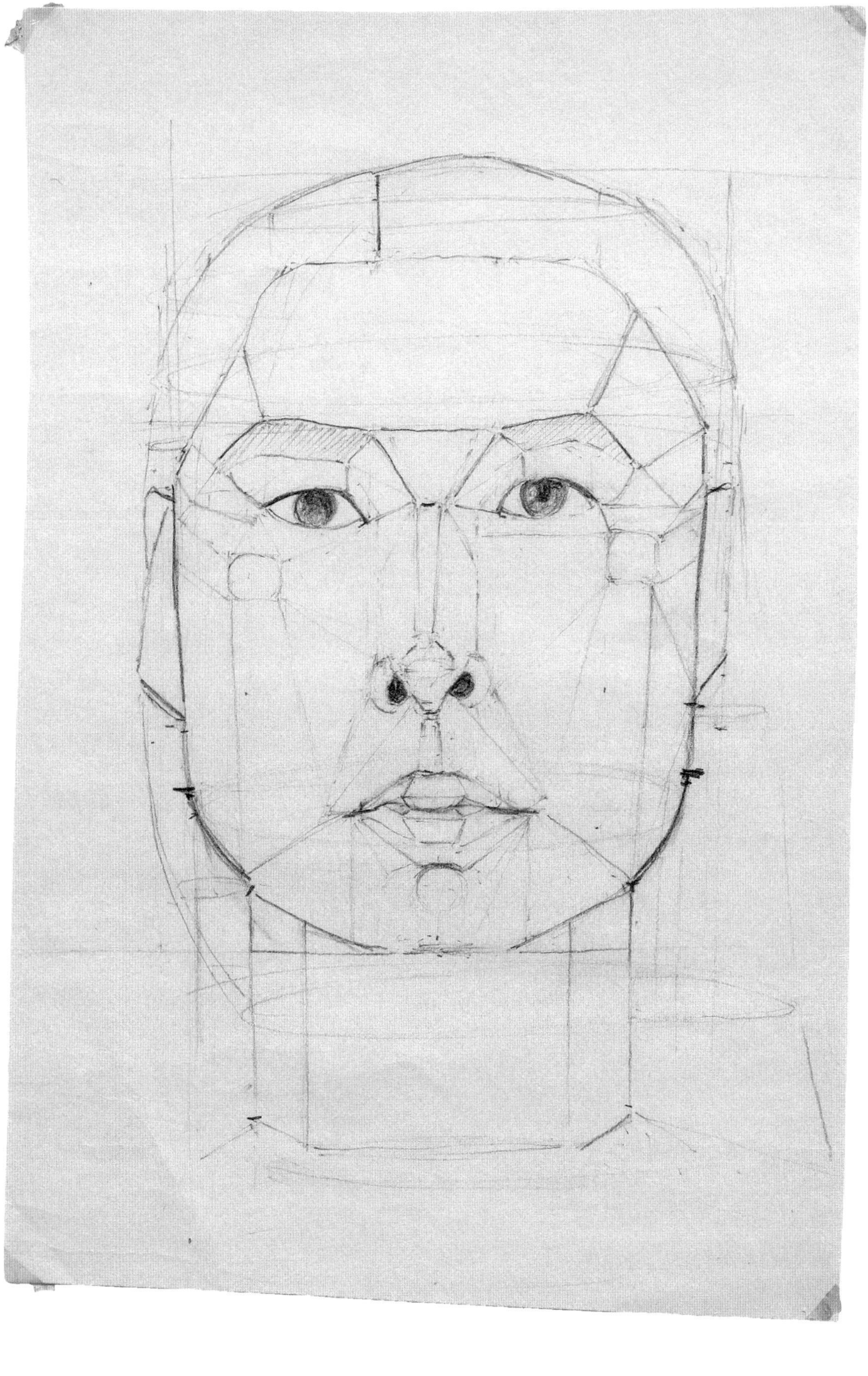

I

The Resurrection of Images

Personal Notes on Pia Arke

Stefan Jonsson

Untitled (Pencil Self-Portrait), c. mid 1980s

Was it in November 1994? The castle's name was Sostrup. A number of young literary scholars from Aarhus University organised a conference that, looking back, seems historic. It was the first time that a considerable group gathered in a Nordic country to discuss postcolonial literature and theory.

On one of the evenings, an artist from the Royal Danish Academy of Fine Arts in Copenhagen gave a performance. Pia Arke sat cross-legged on a table, dressed in a collarless white blouse and khakis, with a packet of tobacco on her lap. She rolled a cigarette, smoked and spoke slowly about one of the photographs that she had pinned to the wall next to the table. She rolled another cigarette and spoke about another image. We were spellbound. In personal twists and ten images, composed with precision and the added testimony of pain and loss, the artist had pinned the colonial system to the story of her life and elucidated the shape of the world. What she spoke about was a sketch for a work which went on to become a part of art history, *Nature Morte*, or *Perlustrations* (p. 50-54), as it is sometimes called.

The year before, I had published a book with the title *De andra: Amerikanska kulturkrig och europeisk rasism* (The Others: The American Cultural War and European Racism). I was in Sostrup to give a talk about it. The book was about the cultural debate that emerged in the US when representatives of the country's minority cultures, long marginalised because of discrimination and racism, laid claim to their own stories and demanded their rightful place in US and Western history. The debate featured words like multiculturalism and postcolonialism. A determined experimental aesthetic opened up windows onto unseen parts of society and disrupted the relationship between centre and periphery.

A few months later I interviewed Pia Arke. It was the start of a friendship and collaboration that continued until Pia's death in the spring of 2007. The interview was published in the Swedish daily newspaper *Dagens Nyheter*, as the final episode in a series of articles about postcolonial thought, all of which were illustrated with Pia's photographs. The article was a fitting summary following articles on the likes of Homi Bhabha, Gayatri Spivak, Valentin Mudimbe and Edward Said. The message? You didn't have to go far to see the postcolonial renewal that emerged in artists who, using words and images, charted their place in the gaps between identities. In fact, one of the foremost proponents lived just around the corner, on Nyelandsvej in Frederiksberg, Copenhagen.

"If you ask Danes about Greenland they get a bad conscience", Pia said in the interview. "But that's not because they're ashamed that their country colonised Greenland but because they don't know anything at all about Greenland." She continued: "My images are about the silence that envelops the ties between Greenland and Denmark. I was born into that silence myself. I'm a mongrel. It's probably not a coincidence that I'm drawn to photography, which in a way is the mongrel of the arts."

When Pia shortly thereafter wrote her dissertation, she returned to the interview. She noted ironically that I had written her into the ranks of postcolonial artists. Not that she considered the categorisation to be wrong, but she simply disliked categorisation in general. Instead she found her own label: *ethno-aesthetics*. The term reflected how on the one hand the cultural power structures placed her in the margins, as ethnic, while on the other hand she used the ethnic identity imposed on her as a point of departure for an aesthetic critique of the norms that expected her to cultivate her "Greenlandness", for example by painting polar bears. Pia found a third position, Greenlandic and Danish, but actually neither of the two. Her work is the result of a mobile perspective that charges the relationship among different identities. Her ability to surprise was astounding. Just think of her large pinhole camera: quite literally a camera body. She didn't paint "Seal on an Ice Floe", but "Camel in Snowscape". All in deep earnest and with great playfulness.

Pia was a deconstructor and an iconoclast. If you look more closely at her oeuvre you notice that, strictly speaking, every individual work consists

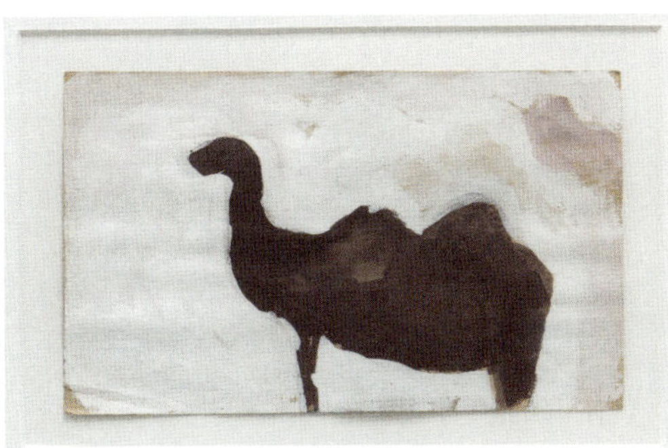

Camel in Snowscape, 1987

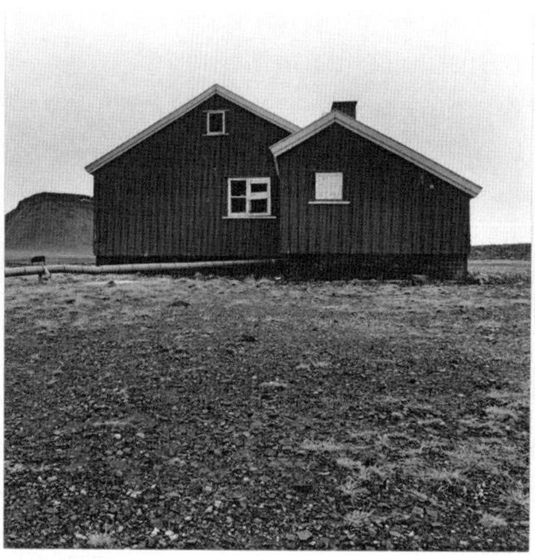

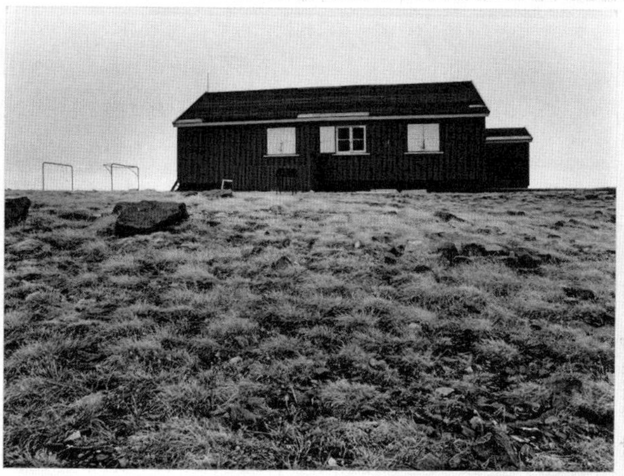

Imaginary Homelands alias *Ultima Thule* alias *Dundas "The Old Thule"*, 1992/2003

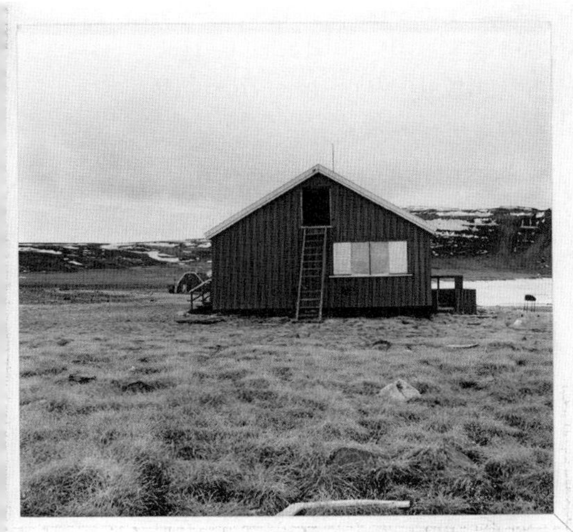

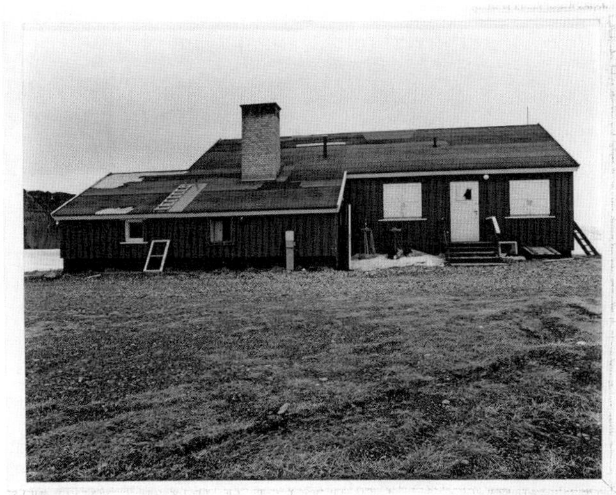

of an image that aims to undermine another, predominant image. That's why she loved the colonial archive, which was like a bottomless reservoir of text and image material just waiting for someone to tear it apart and glue it together anew.

Back to Sostrup. One of the photographs that Pia pointed to depicted a woman looking straight into the camera with a clear, challenging gaze. Her upper body was bare. Where the left breast had once been was now just a rib cage covered in transplanted skin and scar tissue. The surgically removed breast marks the *punctum*, or should we say the *pain spot* of the photograph. The image portraying a person actually depicts something that has been cut away.

Pia said that the portrait was of her friend Susanne Mortensen. She also mentioned that the image had frightened Susanne. Perhaps her fear came from the photograph being so detached and neutral. The cold light, the white background, the frontal camera angle – Pia had used the same techniques as medical photographs of diseases, body parts and medication, or images of scientific racism depicting supposedly "primitive" races. Resting on Susanne's right leg is her breast prosthesis, which she got in order to conceal the absence of what had been cut away.

Pia went on to recount that both she and Susanne were born in Ittoqqortoormiit, or Scoresbysund, in East Greenland, and that Susanne was a qualified "eskimologist", that is, someone who is specialised in the culture of the so-called Eskimos, the indigenous peoples of Greenland and the Arctic.

Pia liked to joke about it: how come the so-called Eskimos became the object of a whole science unto itself? And how do you handle such "knowledge" if you yourself, like Pia and Susanne, belong to those called Eskimos?

Then Pia talked about how the series of images had come about during a time when Pia was driving her friend to her radiation treatment. They wanted to expose something that is often hidden, and thus start a conversation on what is shrouded in silence: How cancer and surgery maim women's bodies; and how colonialism, ethnography and eskimology have severed their connection to their past and their mother tongue.

Pia used to return to a childhood memory sometimes. I like to see it as a code that explains the female figures that populate her work. At times they are surrounded by a strong light, at times by numbing darkness. Pia had a simple way of recounting how she was affected by colonial violence from an early age:

> When I was four we moved to Thule. Sometimes relatives from East Greenland came to visit. I remember lying in bed late at night and listening to them as they sat around the kitchen table and my mother using another voice to speak a language I didn't understand.

The trails of silence led Pia back to Ittoqqortoormiit, a place she had left at the beginning of the 1960s when the family had moved to Thule (her father was a telegraphist), and which she only revisited in 1997 when she took up contact with one of her brothers in her place of birth. She noted that the town had been robbed of its history. In a letter that she wrote after her "homecoming", Pia remarked that funnily enough the history of Scoresbysund was located outside Scoresbysund: "It has moved away and spread to image archives, scientific papers, diaries, attics and cellars in Denmark, Paris, New York, Oslo and Stockholm!"

From this observation the book and art project *Scoresbysundhistorier* (Stories from Scoresbysund) was born, which she asked me to contribute to. I was to tell a story from above – about how explorers and cartographers from different ages have imagined and charted Scoresbysund and East Greenland, about how their maps in turn led to new conquests, which created new maps that guided new expeditions in an unending chain of events. Bit by bit the slow accumulation of facts and observations marked out the place on the world map. Pia's story was about how Greenlanders had modified this place. They had trodden trails and built houses. They had hunted, secured a livelihood for themselves, and formed daily habits and routines. Thus, they had managed to survive and by surviving they had transformed the place into their world.

We met in the Greenlandic village in the summer of 1998. On the second day Pia took me on a hike. Her son, Søren, eight years old at the time, was playing at a cousin's house. Pia liked to work like this – with walks, bike rides and excursions that enabled long conversations, or else sitting around a table discussing images and paging through books. Now we walked on the bay where the meltwater ran in narrow rivulets on the ice. Pia spoke of trauma. "Nobody in Ittoqqortoormiit wants to talk about the past," she said, "about the actual conditions their parents and grandparents faced ... Why they were duped or lured into moving here. How difficult life became. How the children starved, became malnourished, sick and sometimes died. How the men disappeared when they were out hunting on unfamiliar ice. It must come out", Pia added. "Otherwise the silence moves on into the future." And with this she had also explained what our book would be about.

When Pia visited Stockholm about a year after the trip to Ittoqqortoormiit, I took her to *Dagens Nyheter's* image archive – cabinet upon cabinet filled with manila envelopes. We opened a few envelopes marked "Grönland – Folktyper" (Greenland – Racial Types) at random. Pia immediately grabbed hold of a photograph from 1932 of a man and a woman that looked like they were on an evening walk. The man had a knitted sweater, the woman an anorak made of plaid wool with a broad sealskin hem. Both of them looked grumpy, impatient, as if they were just waiting for the photographer to finish. On the back of the photo was a stamp that indicated the copyright as belonging to *The Times* along with the bland note: "Eskimos that the expedition encountered on the way to the base."

"These are Niels and Katinka, my maternal grandparents", Pia exclaimed. She explained that no less than three ships anchored at Scoresbysund in the summer of 1932. They carried European scientists, journalists and tourists. "The locals must have spent a lot of time being photographed. But I've never seen this picture of Grandma and Grandpa."

I nodded. Pia carefully placed the photograph in a folder and stowed it in her rucksack. A bit of stolen history returned to its owner.

It must have been that same summer that she took me down to the storeroom in the back yard on Nyelandsvej. She was eager to show me her new work, the largest she had produced since the actual pinhole camera. She extracted a thick cardboard cylinder, unscrewed the lid and out of its innards she pulled five enormous collages. The series *Legend I–V* (pp. 93-97) is now part of the Louisiana's collection: at the bottom a Danish map, or to be more exact the geological map of East Greenland published in 1971 by the Commission for Scientific Studies in Greenland, on top of it photographs of people from Ittoqqortoormiit, on top of that a transparency with Danish names in red, and lastly a layer of matter – sugar, coffee, rice, oatmeal and flour, to be precise.

I don't remember how Pia explained her work when she spread out the image sheets on the pavement, but she snickered when she saw how the sugar and coffee powder came off the surface when we rolled them up. "It's good when images live and change."

Pia had an odd ability. Behind every image she saw another hidden image which could be drawn out, as long as one knows which technique to use. She had almost the same sensibility for texts: the art of reading between the lines. She even practiced this ability in conversations – what was left unspoken was as significant as what was said. It was an aesthetic and artistic attitude that permeated other areas of life and found expression in a moral and political approach. Or simply put: knowledge of human nature. She understood people's silences and losses.

It is true, she was a destroyer of images, but she was also a restorer, who scraped away at the images of power in order to expose the contours of the people hidden beneath. Thus, she created visual depictions of the pain of the past. Her entire practice was a developing bath. When Pia fixed the image, life came back, resurrected.

Translated by Bettina Schultz

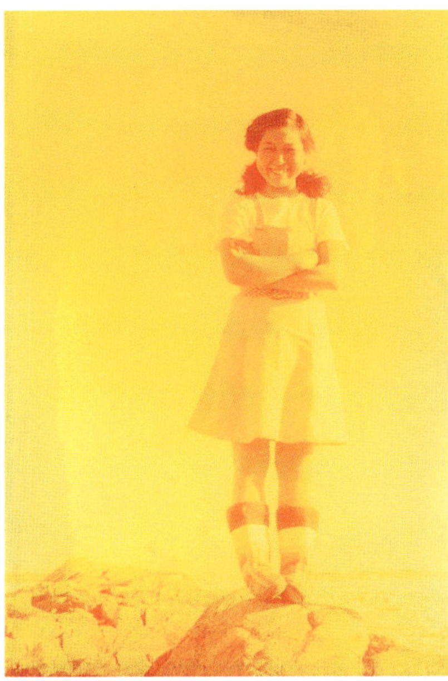

Scoresbysund 1947, c. 1995

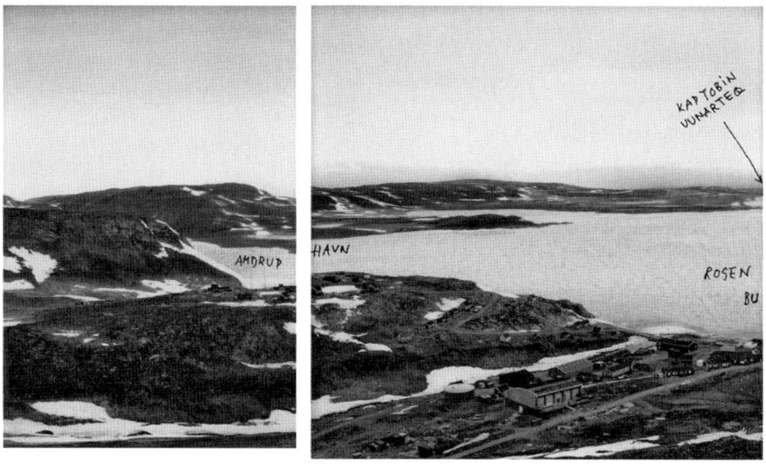

Untitled (Scoresbysund panorama), c. 1997-2001

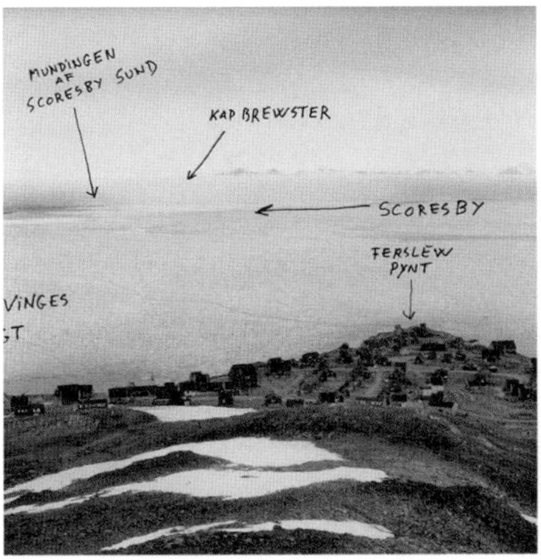
MUNDINGEN AF SCORESBY SUND
KAP BREWSTER
SCORESBY
FERSLEW PYNT

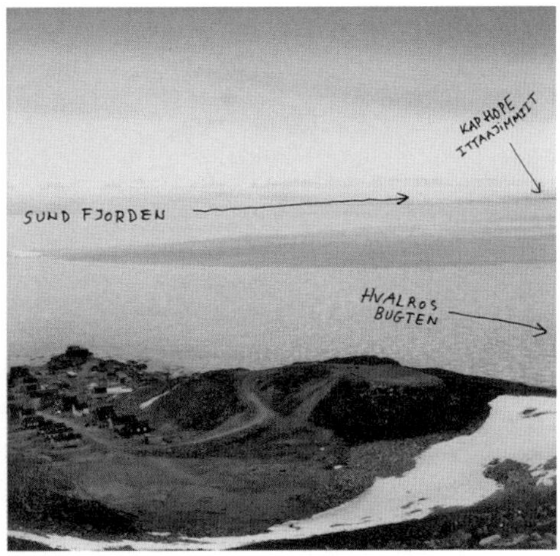
KAP HOPE ITTAAJIMMIIT
SUND FJORDEN
HVALROS BUGTEN

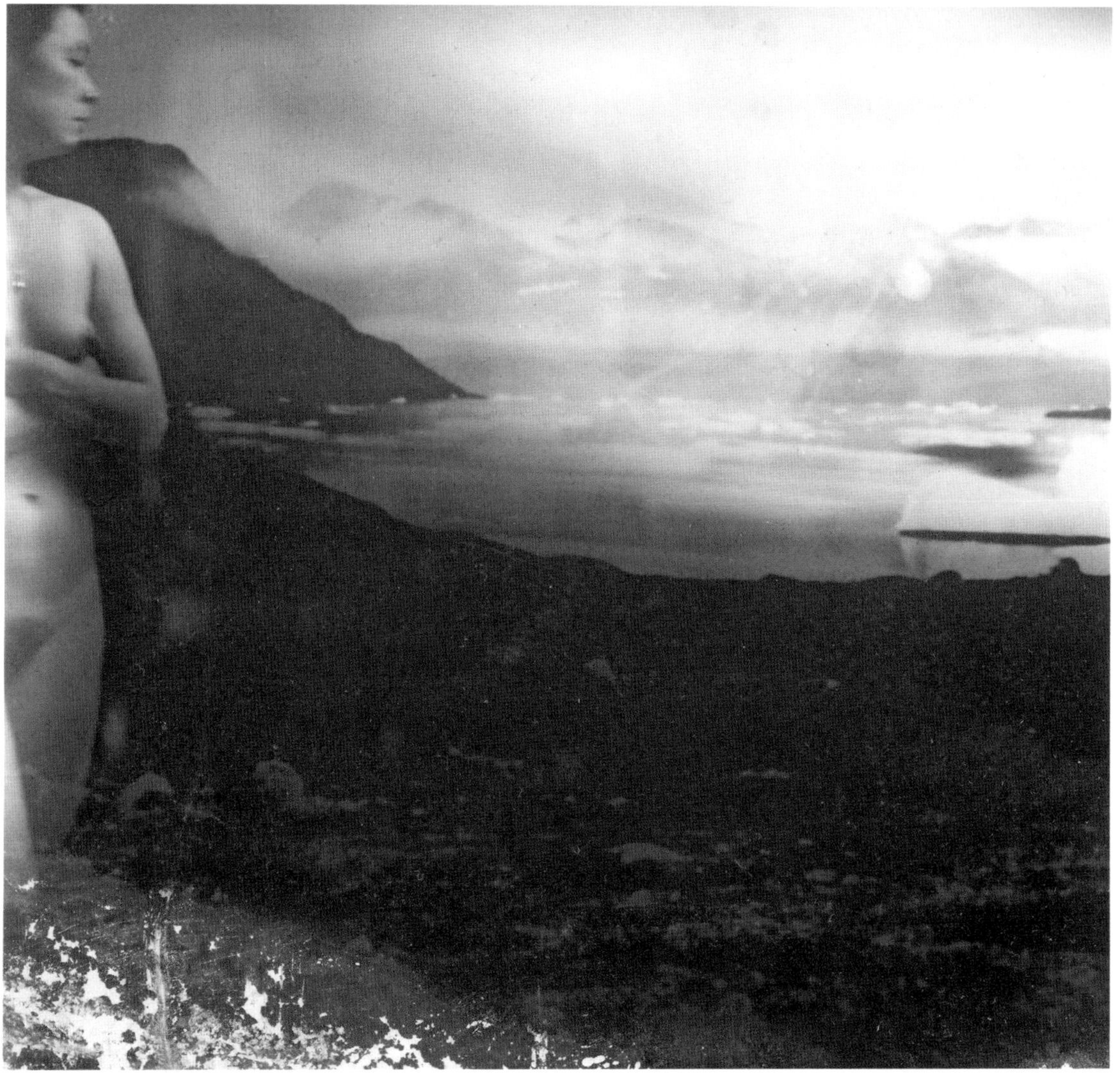

Self-Portrait, 1992

II

The Arctic Portal

Four Years That Took Pia Arke's Art to a Different Place

Anders Kold

An early sequence of self-portraits shows the artist in a corner with a wicker chair and a cabinet of stuffed birds. In the first photo, she is fully dressed. In the following ones, she strikes different poses undressed. In the final one, she has left the picture – only the interior remains. The artist's body later becomes a central motif in her art, with the landscape of Greenland serving as a backdrop for her photographs.

At her untimely death in 2007, Pia Arke left behind a body of work that could fit in a single suitcase. Because so little is known about her early work, the general impression of her career as an artist is based on no more than 15 years in all. All the more reason, then, to zero in on those points in time where her work really takes off. One such period is the four short years when Arke, employing simple photographic techniques and a series of performative "situations", transports herself from a wicker chair in a Copenhagen apartment to a spot overlooking Greenland's drifting icebergs and snow-speckled mountains. What happened?

In a small group of works from 1992, the artist portrays herself "on the ice" (pp. 20, 42 and 82). From this point on, her work is almost continuously bound up with images of the Greenlandic landscape, photographs and maps. This is also when the reception history sets in. *Tupilakosaurus,* a 2010 exhibition at Copenhagen's Den Frie, largely framed Arke's work as the product of her, in many ways, challenging biological position between Denmark and Greenland, as the daughter of a Danish father and a Greenlandic mother. At the time, more than a decade ago, the exhibition clearly aimed to define Arke as an artist who, setting her sights on Greenland, early on pointed her work in a political direction with a postcolonial gaze rooted in artistic research.[1] Indeed, she was speaking from such a position in 2003, when she published her book *Stories from Scoresbysund,* and likely for some years before that, as well. The point is that the hot potato here, of course, is identity. All artists are concerned with identity, but in Arke's early work, before she had set her sights on anything else, this theme can more accurately be described as a process of exploring several different identities and visualities – that is, with no real political objective. Taking a cue from literary theory, we might say that Arke, even back then, was practicing a kind of "performative

Untitled (Self-Portrait, Undressing in Interior), c. 1989

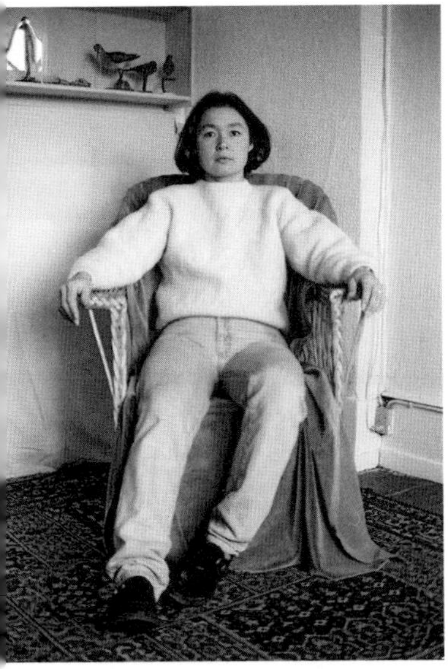
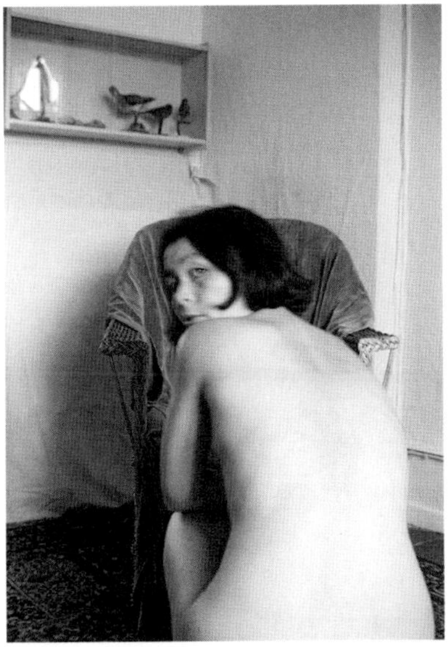
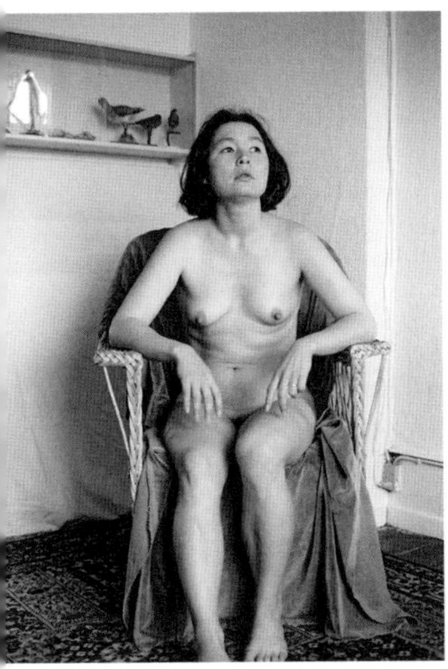
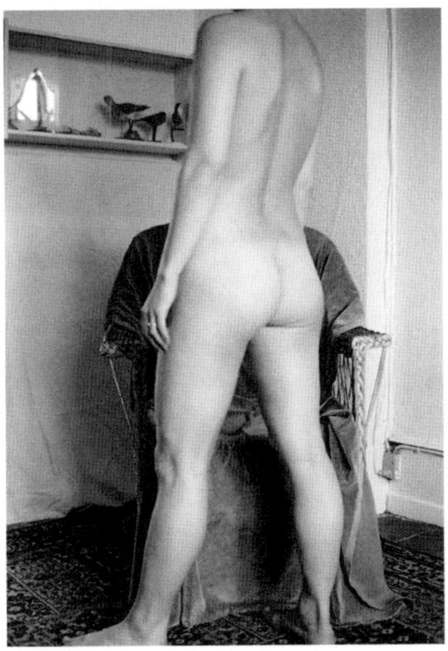
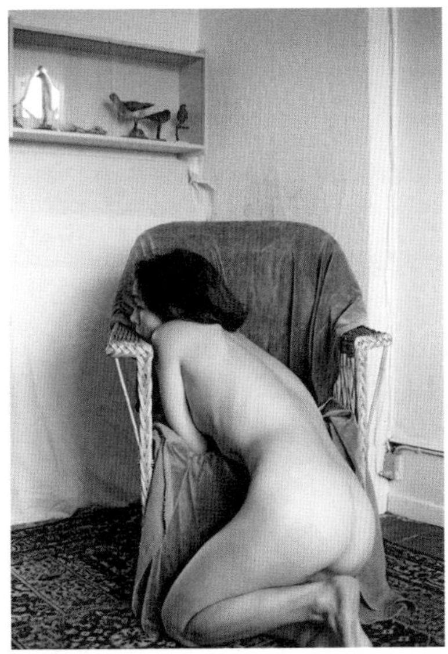
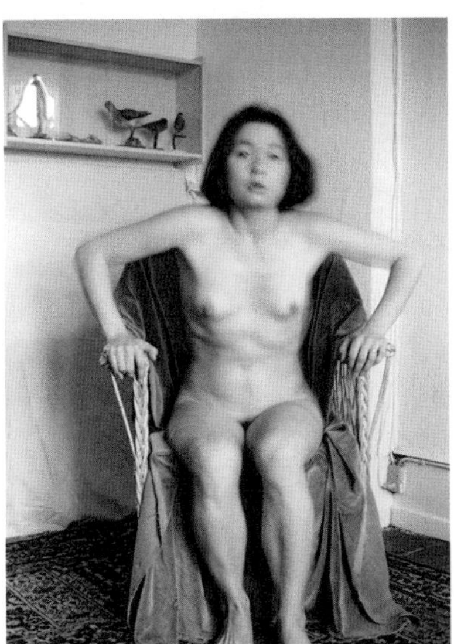
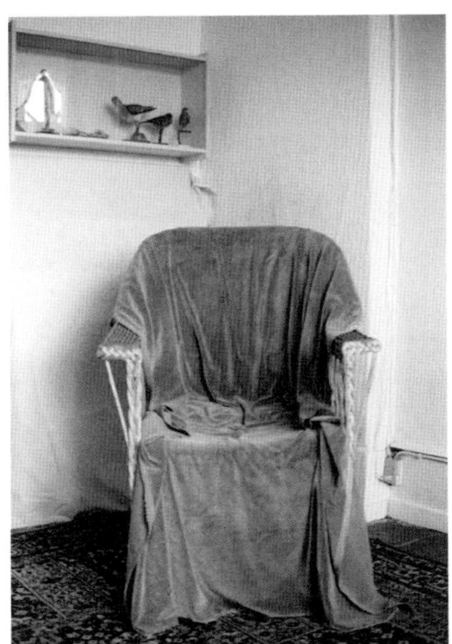

biographism,"[2] staging her photography with an openness that would later enable it to activate other agendas and draw on insight from other fields of knowledge. Still, as late as 1999, the artist stated in an interview, "I'm probably in the aesthetic space of images. I don't see my project as political. If it were, I would just stop making pictures and go out and speak more and write a lot more."[3]

Temporarily parking the determining political perspective and allowing aesthetic reflection, it is evident that Arke took an experimental and very handheld approach, articulating an artistic language that she used to speak to the world ever since. That she did not speak Inuit surely spurred her search, as this lack of language proficiency prompted her to reflect on her identity between two cultures. This much is certain: halfway through art school, Arke was unable clearly to articulate how to fit her biographical roots into a highly performative conceptual photography and, in turn, acquire a political theme. At the time, Arke could best be described as an artist whose relationship to painting was somewhat unstable, as if interrogating her identity could not find original expression in that medium. In 1988, when she moved away from painting and became a denizen of the Royal Danish Academy's Laboratory of Drawing and Photographic Technique under the direction of the artist Per Bak Jensen,

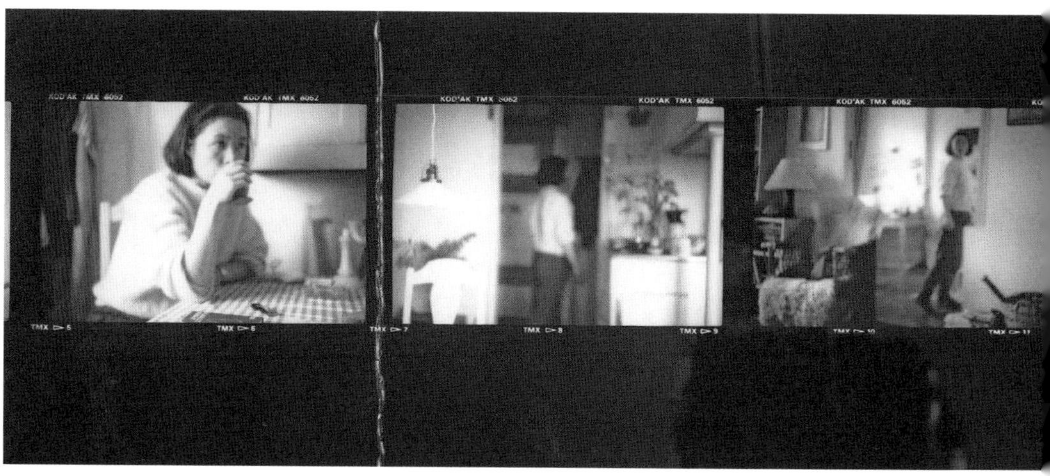

Untitled (Leporello Self-Portrait), c. 1987

her work with the pinhole camera became a house, a portal, which she entered and from which she emerged a few years later to once again put her feet on the ground and look out on the lost land of her childhood.

PHOTOGRAPHIC SEQUENCES

Around 1989, early on in a run of photos anticipating her future work, are a number of sequences are devoted to everyday life – commonplace actions, as one is titled. The works are related by how they show very simple situations or mise-en-scènes of the figure of Pia Arke and the artist of the same name – self-portraits, but not just that. Taken with a timer, *Untitled (Leporello Self-Portrait)* and *Untitled (Self-Portrait, Undressing in Interior)* (p. 23) show the artist in her home. The former sequence offers a peek into other rooms of the apartment and shows Arke in everyday clothes. The latter is the one described in the opening of this essay.[4] In these works, Arke is both subject and object, both behind and in front of the camera. This recognition, and its instrumentation, seems to have struck her with such force that she gave up painting almost overnight. Another reason for turning to photography may have been that the war over painting in the 1980s was petering out and, for all intents and purposes, only male painters remained in the limelight.[5]

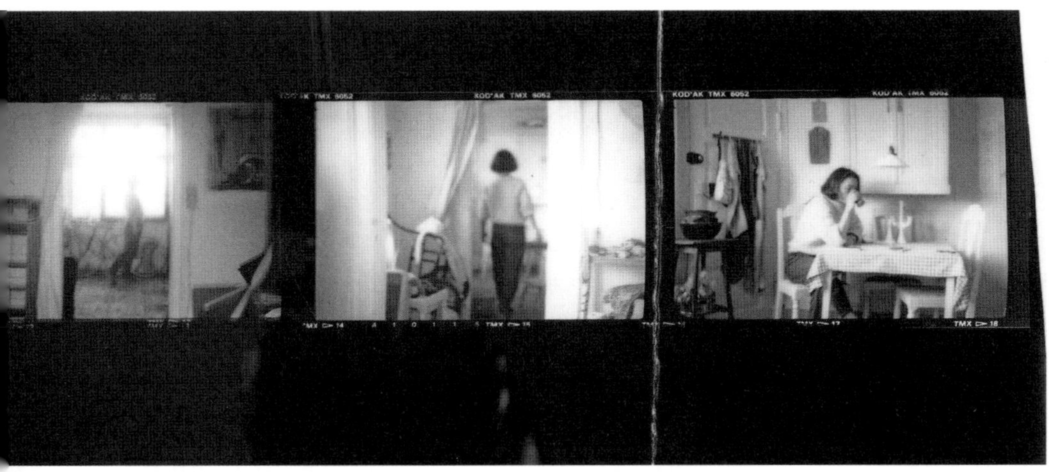

If actions in a social sense are not what we are seeing, what do these series of the artist at home indicate? At play in Arke's works is not self-absorption per se as much as a basic questioning of who she is, where she is from and where she is going – to paraphrase the French painter Paul Gauguin's most famous work. Unlike Gauguin in Haiti, however, Arke has a direct connection to "the original", however troubled it might be. Her biographical core, her "bastard" (Arke's own word) origin between Greenland and Denmark, is put into play.[6] But by concretely looking inward, outward and around, Arke also makes room for others – for us and those who, like herself, want to be several things and in several places at once. In the process, the privacy of the pictures falls away and something transformative takes its place. The Swedish cultural critic Stefan Jonsson, a close friend of the artist, has described how Arke refuses to be in focus and at times even seems to be gesticulating and talking back at us in a language we have yet to learn. That is exactly what makes Arke an artist, not an anthropologist, in those early years. Later, she was only able to question and twist anthropology because she had learned what pictures can do. As I see it, she gains that insight when her thoughts and gaze start revolving around being something else, as well – Pia Arke as multi-dimensional in terms of time, place and persona.[7]

INTIMATIONS

Paraphrasing a familiar subject in the history of art, *Untitled (Self-Portrait, Undressing in Interior)* recalls pictures of artist's studios with female models posed on draped furniture, in various stages of undress – pictured by male artists, of course. Arke's pictures are artful, as well, in the sometimes blurry image quality produced by the timer and the scenographic variations. Apparent crudity or rawness is a thread in all of Arke's work. A perfect finish meant nothing to her. Nor is her art documentarism in the usual sense. On closer inspection, the six small images of the figure and the wicker chair can be seen to make up a performative matrix of sorts for her work up to and including her iconic 1992 self-portraits "on the ice", as well as for a number of major works from the following year. We see her looking straight at us, looking away, sitting down, kneeling and getting up. In profile, too. Replace the apartment in Copenhagen with the backdrop of the Greenlandic landscape three years later, and the nude figures of the artist could practically have been slotted in, as though they were cardboard cutouts, a function of a choreography that today can be seen to support the artist's *in motion* between Copenhagen and the landscape at Narsaq, on the southern tip of Greenland.[8] In her 1992 self-portraits set against a large print of this landscape, the artist is moving, but she is also beginning to set the world in motion. Here, she is performing on a stage that had been marked out and investigated before her mainly by the feminist artists of the late 1960s, and it is unthinkable that she did not navigate by them.[9] She is model, observer and artist at once.

For context, let us turn to the work of another, far better known, woman artist. While Arke may not actually have seen or known the American artist Cindy Sherman's 1975 *A Play of Selves*,[10] performative photography was all the rage in those years. Having abandoned painting herself early on, Sherman made this series of 72 black-and-white photographic tableaus, each no bigger than a sheet of letter-sized paper. The work is based on 245 shots of herself, which she cut out and arranged in scenarios she had detailed in a script – a very cinematic approach

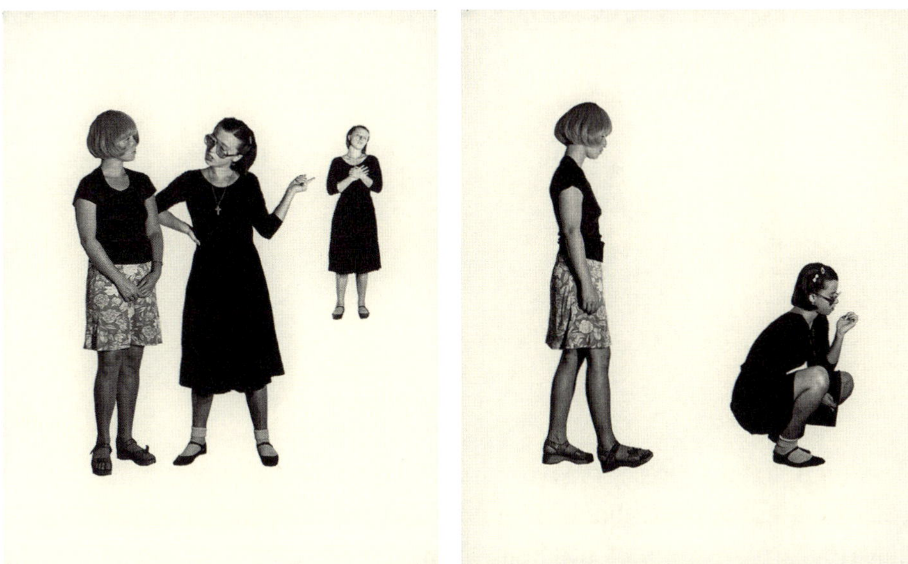

Cindy Sherman: *A Play of Selves (details)*, 1975
72 black-and-white photo collages, various dimensions
Glenstone Museum, Potomac, Maryland

that led to her iconic *Film Stills.*[11] The similarities to Arke's later superimpositions of herself on the Greenlandic landscape are obvious. In this process, both artists, with varying distance to the camera, had to envisage the image through the orientation of the figures. Note that both artists in these early staged works are clearly letting us know that the background, literally, is another film. A similar effect is seen in *Untitled* (1988–89), a series of photos that Arke made in distinctly domestic surroundings, posing a couple of friends in tableaus based on classical art.[12]

As the title implies, Sherman's *A Play of Selves* is about a number of characters (16 in all) within a single individual, acting out theatrically familiar representations of her – as she sees herself, but also very much as her surroundings in a male-dominated popular visual culture see her as a woman. For its part, the figure in Arke's 1992 self-portraits

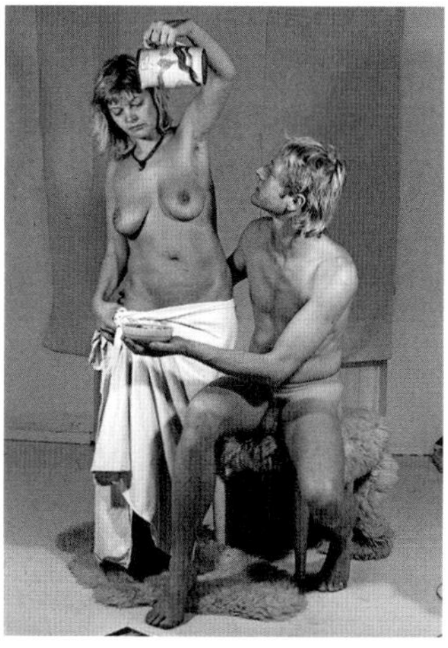

Photo from Pia Arke's archive

is so open that it represents a woman, an artist in a wide open space and a biographical self that is neither Danish nor Greenlandic. The dual device of movement and being moved is what the medium of photography offered Arke, developing her as a person and setting her course as an artist.

A WOMAN VANISHES

Movement, literally expressing the opposite of stasis, is relevant to Arke's art and presents a number of interpretative possibilities. For one, Arke uses shots where artefacts of time are a clearly visible part of the process – moving around in front of the camera, the artist documents the passage of time. The final picture in *Untitled (Self-Portrait, Undressing in Interior)* likewise expresses movement – the movement implied by her absence. She has vanished from the picture. Only an empty chair remains. The following year, she is back in her apartment in Copenhagen,[13] acting out the familiar figurations, this time around a small table and a chair – front, rear, side, standing, seated. In these seven colour photos, the wall behind her in the plain room is decorated with toy masks of (non-arctic) animals and, in one shot, photos of a landscape and map of Greenland.[14] The images in the 1990 series *Untitled (Double Exposure Self-Portrait in Interior)* (p. 88) alternate between presence and more spectral apparitions, while the social space now is all but drained of any hint of commonplace actions – "scenic" is a more descriptive term. This is the last we see of the artist before she leaves for Greenland later that year. Working with a self-made wooden pinhole camera (p. 32) large enough to contain a person, she let the light of Greenland stream in through a tiny hole in the front wall of the box and leave an image of the landscape on the rear wall behind her. The landscape is known from her self-portraits two years later. It took 15 minutes to fix the view on the photosensitive film on the rear wall. Meanwhile, both the landscape and the artist's body moved, as is apparent in several prints of the landscape. Now, she was actually *in* the landscape, though shielded inside the dark room of the box, physically and mentally experiencing a connection across time to the view from her childhood home, with all the thoughts it triggered. "They [these places] have followed me in my memory. They are part of me and my way of seeing and experiencing the world. They have a very clear language that speaks of evolution, oblivion and transience. They remind me of who we are. Which is not always a pleasant thing."[15]

Arke's camera box became an obvious substitute for the house she had lived in as a child in the late 1960s, which was now gone. This meeting of the body and the landscape – or, more accurately, an image of the landscape – remained her chief artistic device right up to and including her 1999 series *Legend I-V* (pp. 93-97). Back at the Academy in Copenhagen, the box had apparently enabled her to grasp how she could be both herself and an "other", while also connecting to the place, Greenland. Arke seems to have used the concrete, physical existence of the box to board a train of thought that took her places. In the same way that she had employed the table and chair in her Copenhagen apartment, she now incorporated an impression of a landscape and, later, maps and other people's pictures of Greenland, as well.

SILENCE AND IMAGES

Returning from her encounter with the view in Narsaq, Arke gave birth to a son, Søren, in November 1990. Thoughts of family and landscapes must surely have occupied her inside the box, as they did in her work ever since. Nor is it likely that Arke stood passively by and let the world work in the picture, and in herself, during the 15-minute exposure. It is also hard to imagine that she did not give a thought to how, in her practice, she could project ideas and thoughts back on the world in order to move it, and herself. The concept of performative biography, mentioned in the opening of this essay, also applies to what we see in Arke's photos from 1992: the artist is in motion, directing her communication in all directions, which includes questioning who is looking at whom. Her nude self-portraits on a landscape background are also, inevitably, about Greenland. In *Self-Portrait with Cousin*, from later that year, it is possible to see an opening to an actual post-colonial imprint on the image. As always, Arke is in motion; it is she who is blurring in and out of focus. But in one place, both women look at us with their arms crossed, against the backdrop of Greenland. Here, Arke is applying the ethnographic gaze she describes in her 1995 thesis *Ethno-Aesthetics*. Contemplating this photo makes you conscious of your own point of view and your view of "others". Arke is putting her identity into play, without freezing the picture. Her brother, Erik Gant, described her method in 1996: "She insists that photography is part of her heritage. And that photo-telegraphy is her method of sending herself 'home' by sending herself in all directions."[16] Their father had worked as a telegraph operator in several locations in Greenland, where he met their mother. There was plenty to talk about. Especially about the "silence", as Arke called it, between the former colonial power of Denmark and a Greenland moving towards self-rule. The pinhole camera – the black box – is an apt metaphor here. Silence cries out for pictures. In 1992, Pia Arke had acquired a fully articulated artistic language with the potential to authoritatively play out a world of identities in images, while also considering the greater world, the relationship between Greenland and Denmark for instance.

Translated by Glen Garner

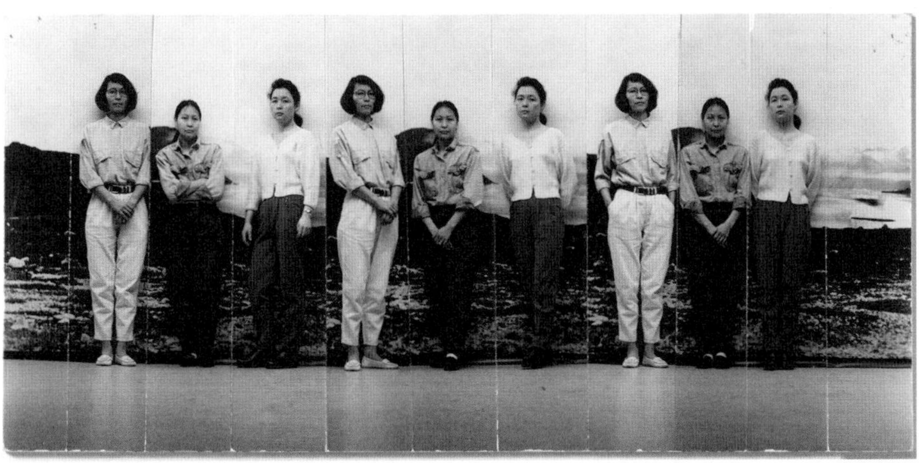

Untitled (The Three Graces Collage), 1994

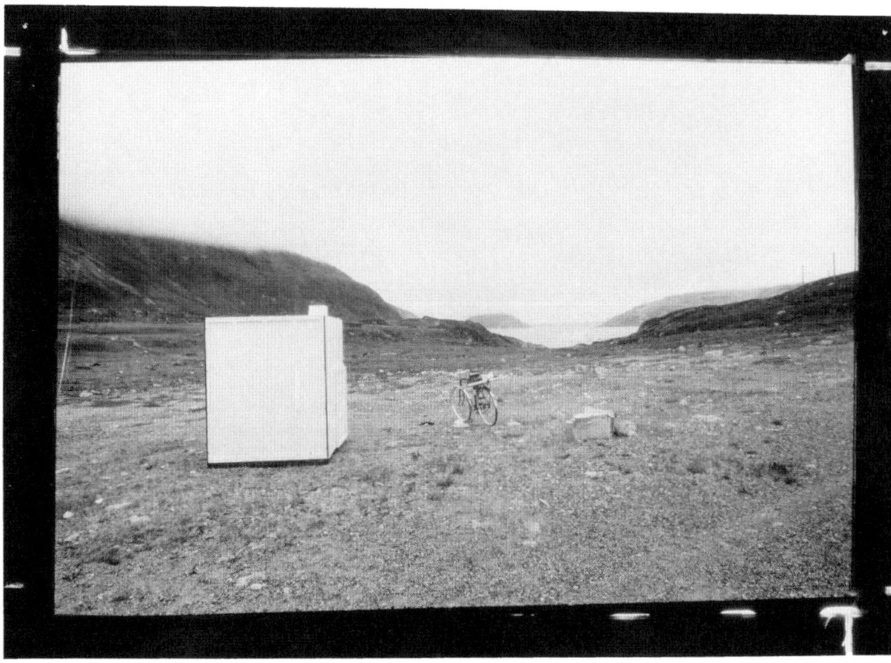

Pia Arke's pinhole camera in Narsaq, photo from the artist's archive

III

Into Photography

Pia Arke and Her Pinhole Camera

Erik Steffensen

Pia Arke was a generous, open and inquisitive artist when I met her in 1987. We were both studying at the Royal Danish Academy of Fine Arts, at the top of a building in the street behind the academy itself. I'd started at the academy the year before, but the first two years were basically general studies, so students from both years were part of the same community. The people we met during that time were who we saw as our generation of artists. We didn't have much to do with the older students, who'd already moved on to schools with professors. Pia, like most of us, had been accepted at the academy as a painter, but it was on courses and trips with the photography lab that her artistic development really took off.

She found an anchor in photography, a place to experiment with herself, her ideas, her body, her history – to make all kinds of investigations in fast, accessible ways. When Pia told us – slightly self-consciously – that she'd sold some watercolours to SAS for brochures on flights between Greenland and Copenhagen, you could sense she was divided. If she continued down that path she would achieve recognition as an artist of sorts, one who could contribute with ethnic specialities, probably limited to painting the kayaks or polar bears of tourist clichés. Which would, of course, have been a way to survive. But maybe abandoning painting in favour of photography was what made it possible to escape the confines of traditional art and approach her own, unique story. Pia discovered photography, or maybe it was photography that discovered her. She made her own analogue photographs, as well as using family snaps and archive material. Photography became her primary medium.

Pia's approach to art was unschooled, and stayed that way. She was not wildly expressive, more quiet, receptive and critical in a subdued way. She was unique. Good company, warm, and helpful too, but not with the usual 'I'll scratch your back if you scratch mine' attitude of a lot of the other students. She wasn't calculating, and was liberatingly free of artistic pretensions. She was ambitious, but ambitious for the work rather than herself. Work that was her own story – and history. She experimented with instant Polaroid cameras, where the image appeared virtually as soon as you pressed the button, performed role play in front of the lens, and experimented in every thinkable direction. One day we started working with pinhole cameras. Pia chose to make a totally original and impossible model. She made a box she could actually get inside, then had it transported

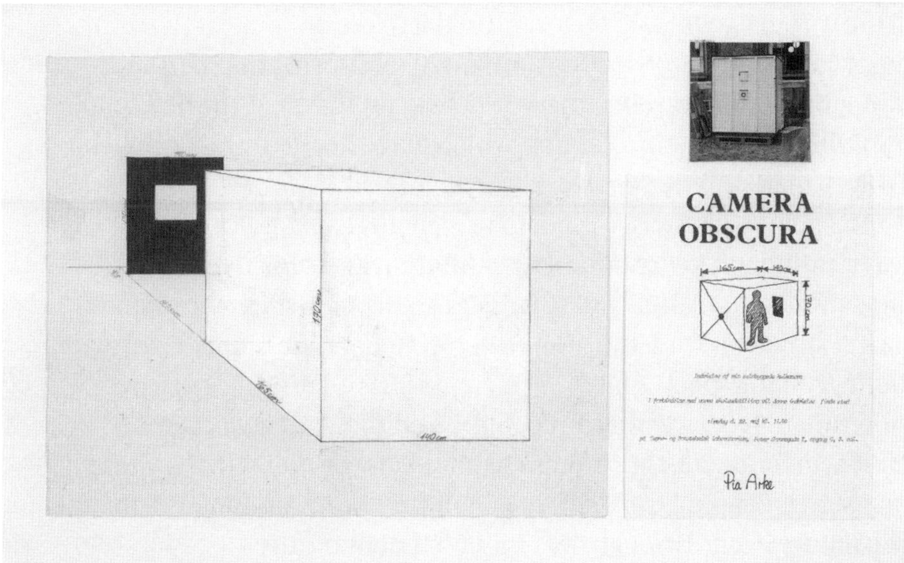

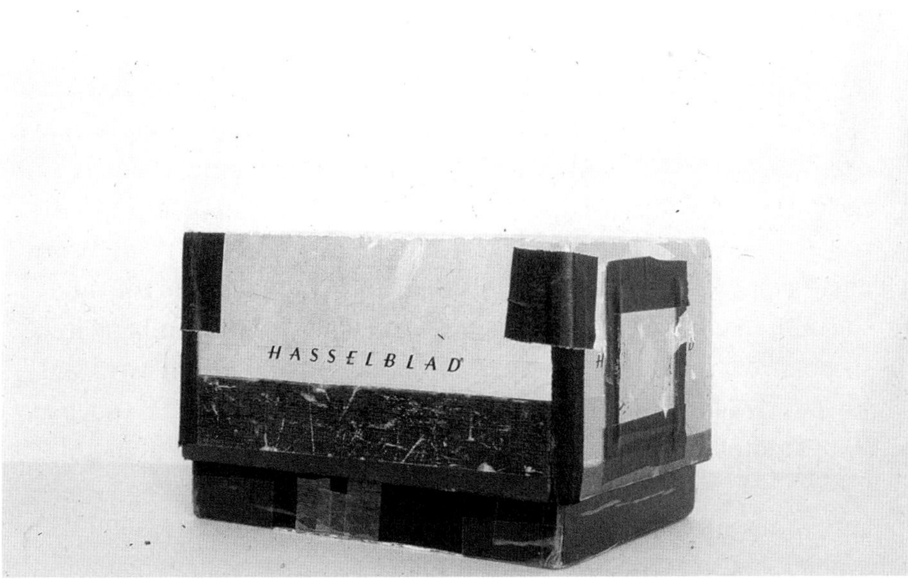

Top: *Untitled (Drawing Plan for Large Camera Obscura*, 1990, *Untitled (Camera Obscura)*, 1990 and *Camera Obscura*, 1990

Bottom: *Untitled (Small Camera Obscura)*, 1988-1990

all the way to Greenland. Here she used it to create some of the most important photographs to see the light of day during that period. Photographs that travelled the world, reaching as far as the newspaper *Frankfurter Allgemeine Zeitung*, which led to her getting to know the Zurich gallerist Irène Preiswerk.

The point of this story is not to present a survey of Pia Arke's oeuvre, although her spontaneity – different and sensitive as it was – and experiments raised and still raise important issues. With limited means, she created a setup, filmed herself lying naked and performed *Arctic Hysteria* (p. 38), and took photographs of immense beauty and authenticity. Her style was direct. She just did it. And it worked. She was fearless in following the impulse behind her works and in the works themselves. Leaping from cliff to cliff in Kullen, it was in nature that her own nature shone through. As a fellow student recalls:

> Pia started at the academy the same year as me, in 1987. I saw a photograph by Sally Mann the other day, and remembered the time in the photo lab when Pia said she found [Mann] was interesting. I said – ironically really – that she should just write to her, then the two of them could become pen pals. Fourteen days later she said "Thanks for the tip. We're writing to each other now, and she's sent me some photographs" ... Another time, when she was struggling with copying images for an exhibition, I said: "I'm better at printing than you, so just call the curator and say you need someone to print for you and that it costs." She did it immediately. No problem. And the time she built that huge *camera obscura* she could get inside and had it shipped to Greenland. Not many of us thought that would work. But we found out that maybe we over-thought things, and that if you give things a shot they sometimes work out.

It's something Bill Gates always says: Don't put anything off. It might seem naïve and reckless to throw yourself into life and art by following such simple advice, but for Pia it was a model that worked. She thought things through as she sat rolling one of her cigarettes. Her open face and intense presence stand clearly in my memory. And throughout her entire oeuvre.

Translated by Jane Rowley

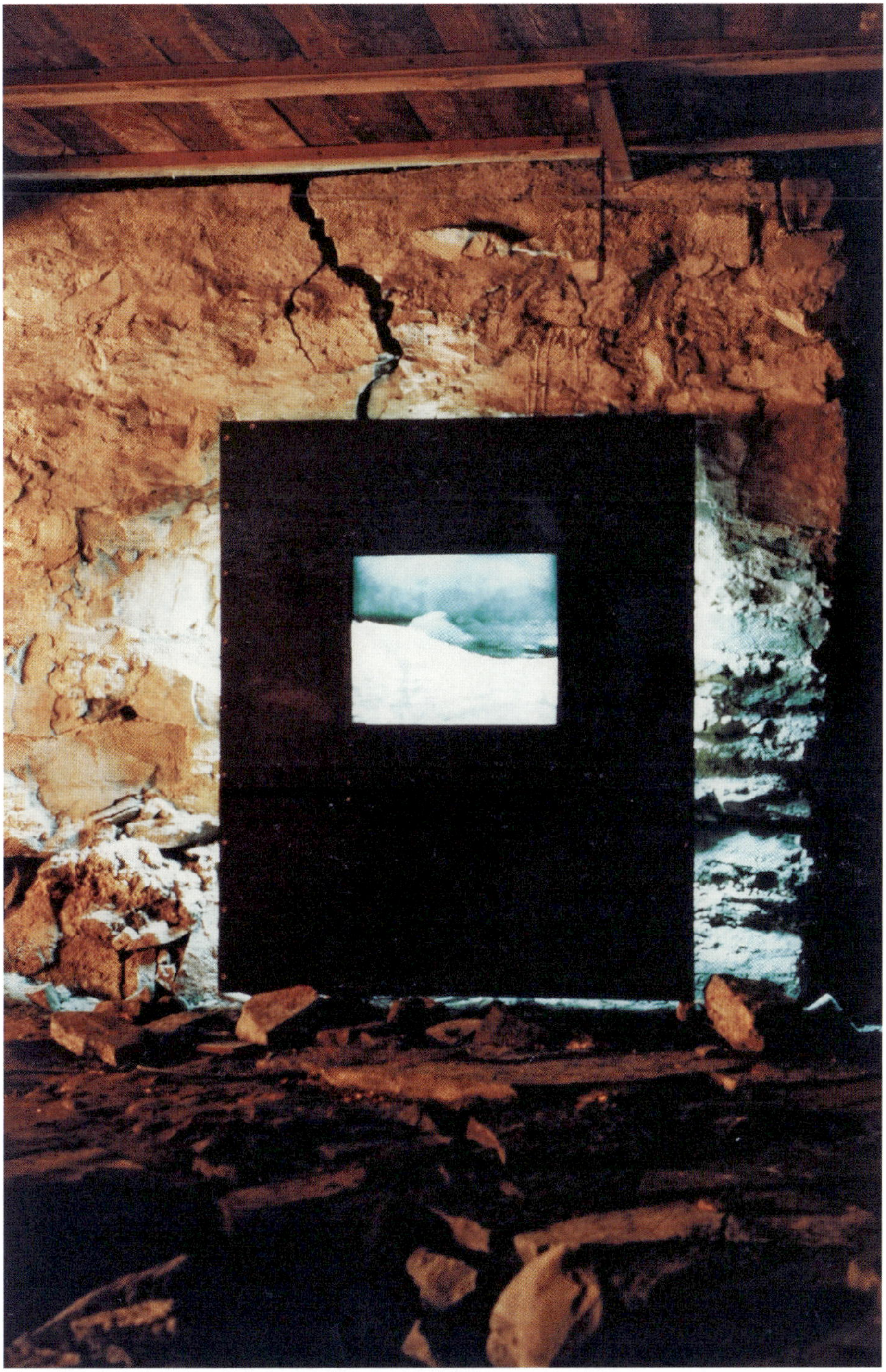

Untitled (Pinhole Camera Negative), c. 1992

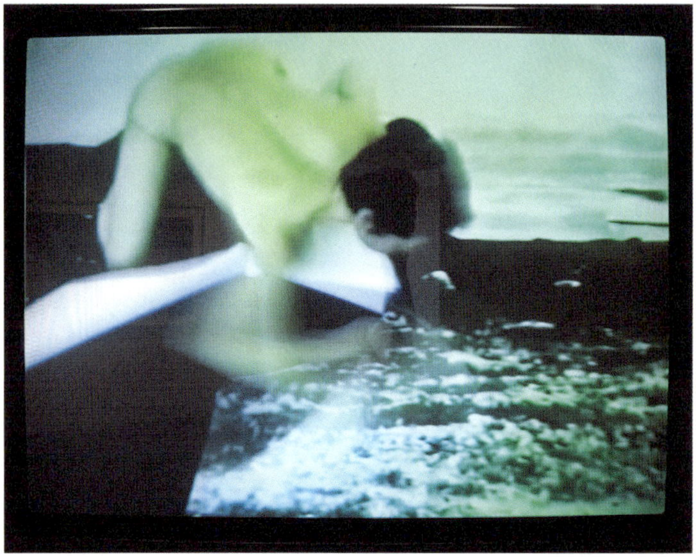

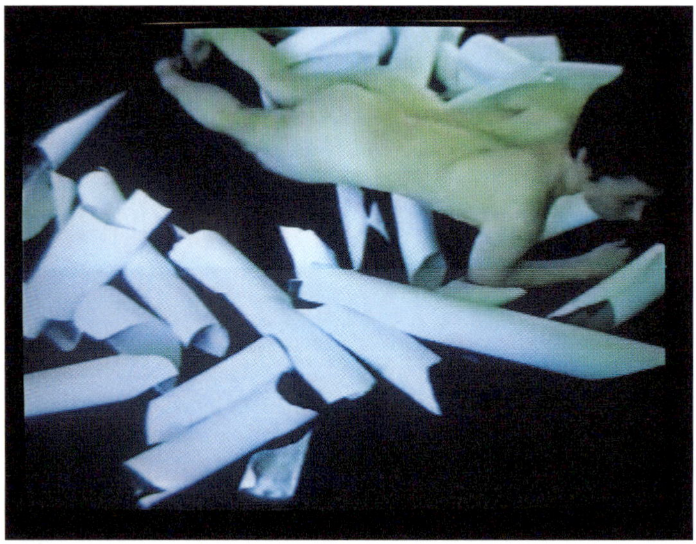

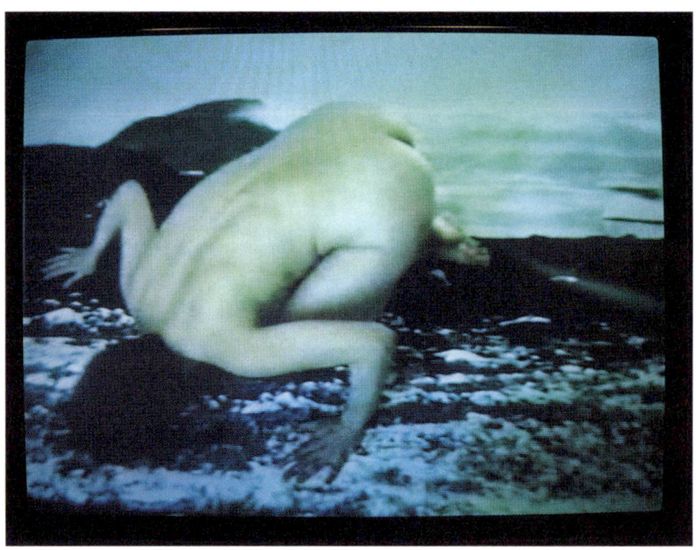

IV

For Those Who Live on the Shoreline:

Notes on Pia Arke's *Arctic Hysteria*

Laura Smith

Stills from *Arctic Hysteria*, 1996

It was odd, she thought, how if one was alone, one leant to things, inanimate things; trees, streams, flowers; felt they expressed one; felt they became one; felt they knew one, in a sense were one.[1]

Virginia Woolf

In her video performance *Arctic Hysteria* (1996) (p. 38), Pia Arke crawls naked across a giant black-and-white photograph of Nuugaarsuk Point, a spit of land in the southern archipelagos of Greenland. The performance consists of almost one single scene, save for an opening shot of Arke's studio, revealing a wonky flash of domesticity. Nuugaarsuk Point, outside the small town of Narsaq, is where Arke lived and grew up in the 1960s. In the video, we zoom in on the photograph of the landscape until it fills the shot, at which point Arke enters from the right, crawling on to the image steadily and intently. She stalls, pauses, she sniffs at the ground, breathes it in, she strokes it, almost caresses it. She lies down, she swims on top of the image, she turns on to her back, stretches out, presses herself into the paper, she rolls, strokes, smells again. Then she begins to tear the image; she tears it in swathes, creating curls of white paper that – as she slowly and methodically pulls apart the image – form a sea of torn forms around her until she then departs, crawling out of shot to the right of the frame. The entire performance lasts a concise six minutes with the only sound being the noises, recorded in real time of Arke's body grappling with the paper. The performance is tender; the tearing is loving, not destructive, and the intimacy of the scene alongside the title's colonial allusions create a highly charged atmosphere. An important addition to Arke's body of work, the video also makes a powerful contribution to discourse around the representation of indigenous peoples, colonial power and the role of a woman's body, both historically and geographically.

Arke was the daughter of an Inuit seamstress, Birgitte Justine Piparajik Arqe, and Danish telegraphist Jørgen Gant. She was born in 1958 in Ittoqqortoormiit (or Scoresbysund), Denmark's outermost colonial settlement in East Greenland. During her childhood, Arke and her family (she had three siblings) moved frequently, settling in various Danish outposts around Greenland as a result of her father's job. This itinerant upbringing granted her an understanding of the processes at work in Denmark's colonisation of Greenland as well as a tangible awareness of the landscapes of her country. One such landscape was Nuugaarsuk Point where, in her adult years, Arke would return to set up a large, handcrafted pinhole camera (big enough for her to climb inside) to document the landscape around her childhood home. It is one of these pinhole images that she shares the ground with in *Arctic Hysteria*.

From her birth, throughout her childhood and adolescence, and through to her studies at The Royal Danish Academy of Fine Arts, Arke was caught within the imperial and colonial complexities of Danish rule in Greenland and used her mixed ethnicity to pose questions about how history is created, to whom it belongs, and what happens to a place and its people when foreign powers assume control over the ways that it is represented. Equally significant, though, are Arke's explorations of the role of women within this complicated field. In *Arctic Hysteria,* naked and vulnerable, she uses her body to mimic the movements of the explorer, the colonist, the discoverer, but with a far more instinctual and intuitive energy that celebrates both her indigeneity and her identity as a woman. As Kuratorisk Aktion, a radical feminist curatorial collective who curated the first retrospective of Arke's work, state: "colonialism's most important ideological form of oppression is not only racism but also the special form of sexism contained in the act of hyper-feminising the ethnic woman."[2]

In 1995, while carrying out research in the archives of the Explorers Club in New York, Arke came across the collection of Robert E. Peary, the North American explorer who in 1909 (falsely) claimed he had reached the North Pole. In Peary's collection, Arke found a photograph of a naked, screaming Inuit woman restrained before the camera by two white men.

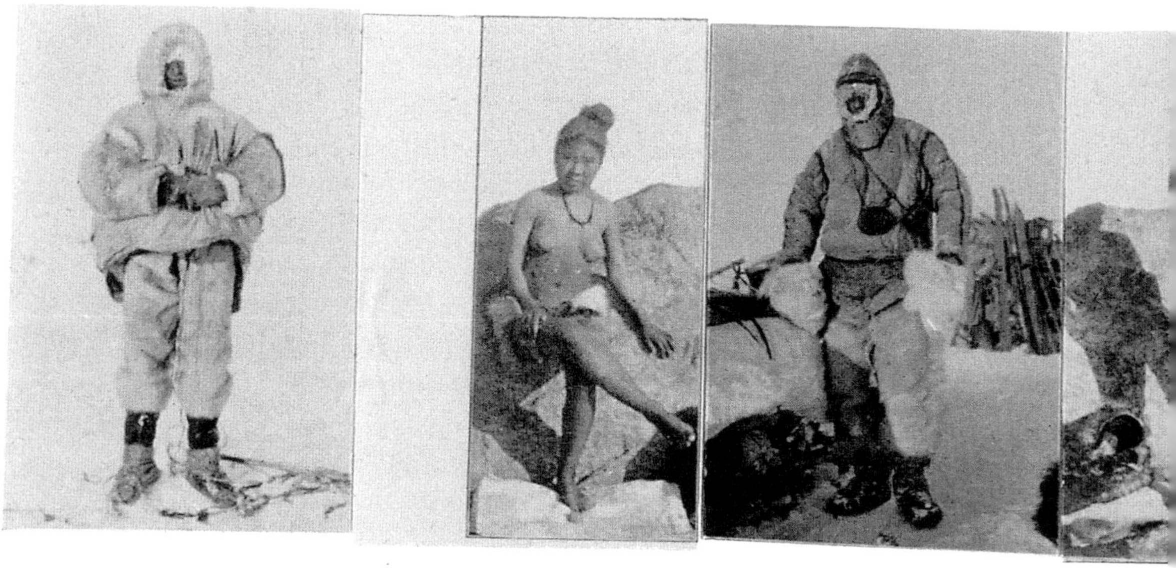

Arctic Hysteria IV, 1997

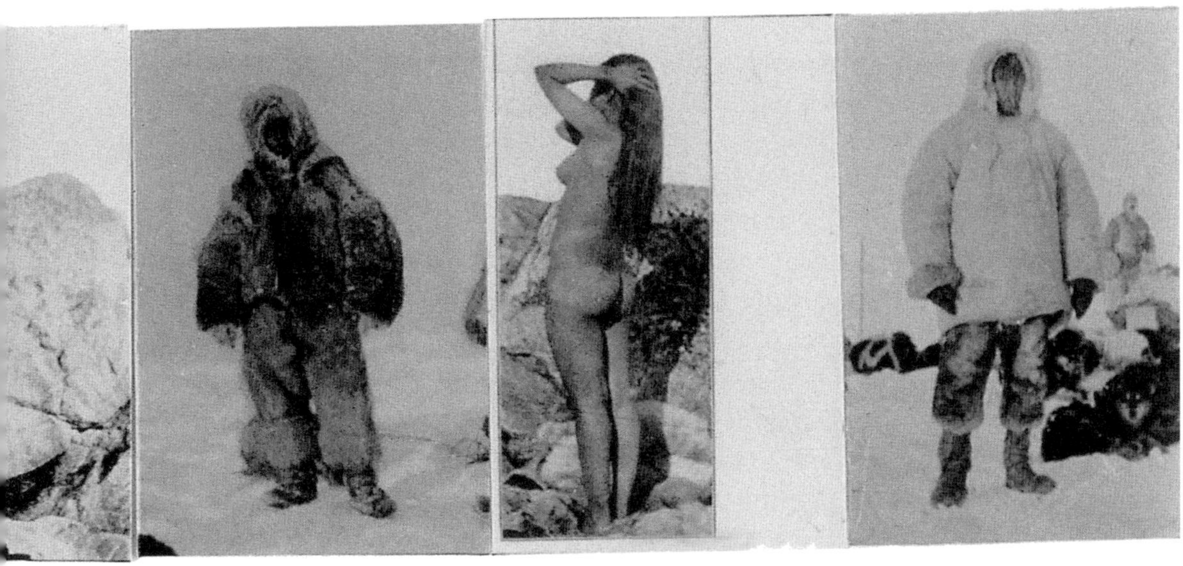

The archivist informed Arke that the woman was suffering from 'Arctic hysteria', a mental disorder, also known as Pibloktoq that was concocted in the 1910s largely based on Peary's accounts of Inuit women suffering fits of rage, and wild and ferocious behaviour. Despite the fact that Peary had no psychiatric or medical training, his theories dovetailed perfectly with the field's turn-of-the-century beliefs in the intrinsic weakness of the female mind and the essential primitivism of non-white peoples. As a result western psychiatrists and physicians of the period were fascinated by Peary's accounts, and scientific careers were built on the mental and physical abuse of Inuit women. Photographs such as Peary's, which introduced the Arctic people to southerners, frequently depicted Inuit women as hysterical or hypersexual. During her investigations into 'Arctic hysteria' Arke created a photographic work called *Arctic Hysteria IV* (pp. 42-43), which juxtaposed portraits appropriated from Peary's 1898 book *Northward over the 'Great Ice'* showing Peary and his three expedition members Clark, Baldwin and Entrikin, in full explorer attire, with three unnamed Inuit women in the nude, revealing the gross power imbalances at play between coloniser and colonised.

The othering of a woman, particularly an Indigenous woman, is historically no surprise. In *Arctic Hysteria,* Arke reclaims both her own body and her own landscape. Landscape is an important metaphor for freedom and power beyond the realms of existing and oppressive cultures. As Catherine Clément and Hélène Cixous assert in *The Newly Born Woman*: "there is a voice crying in the wilderness – the voice of a body dancing, laughing, shrieking, crying. Whose is it? The voice of a woman, newborn and yet archaic, a voice of milk and blood."[3] It is through landscape, then, that women might harness the possibilities for a future self that is outside of existing societal bounds. These possibilities, which rebuff cultural stereotypes around gender and race, are attached to the unknown and the wild. That is not to say that 'woman' herself is wild – or that 'woman' equates in any way with 'nature' – but rather that articulating a desire for woman's sexual, social and artistic freedom depends on exploring something that is not yet known: "somewhere every culture has an imaginary zone for what it excludes."[4] This sense of dispossession, but burgeoning hope in the unknown, finds resonance in the words of Audre Lorde:

For those of us who live at the shoreline
standing upon the constant edges of decision
crucial and alone
for those of us who cannot indulge
the passing dreams of choice
who love in doorways coming and going
in the hours between dawns
looking inward and outward
at once before and after
seeking a now that can breed
futures[5]

These tremendously moving words, in turn, resonate with Arke's actions and entire oeuvre. The landscape, the shoreline, for her, is both the backdrop and the starting point for navigating her relationship between Denmark, Greenland and her own body, and the voices that her works amplify show landscape to be changeable and malleable according to who is speaking. The result is a body of work that reveals new spaces, new possibilities and new futures for those who have been excluded. In *Arctic Hysteria*, Arke's performance troubles the notion of the colonial master and the exhibited native in a way that means neither may reassume their previous positions without question. Like an archaeologist, she digs herself into her past and her land. And in so doing she brings her challenges into dialogue with her own body. As she states: "I make the history of colonialism part of my history in the only way I know, namely by taking it personally."[6]

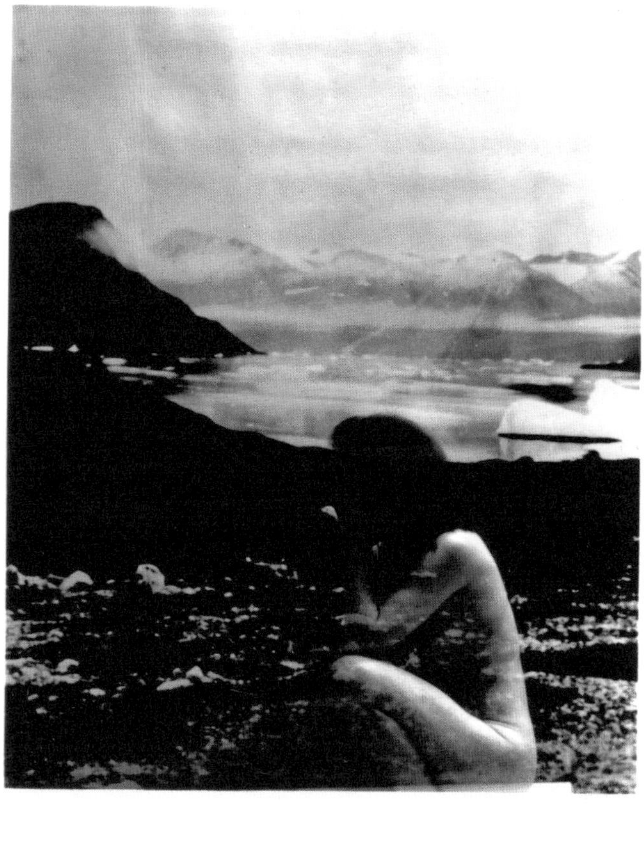

Self-Portrait, 1992

V

Still Life

Kim Leine

Nature morte. The silence of the photograph is painful. People who were once alive, moments that have passed, captured by the dead blink of a lens. Book spines with faded titles on a dusty shelf. An anxious gaze levelled through a pair of glasses. The scarred skin of a mastectomy; an absence of topography and flesh. Past and present. Life stopped mid-movement, suspended in the developing tray. Gone. Moments frozen forever. Death-mask faces. Unable to move. Unable to move on. Capable only of being beheld and interpreted. Photography is perhaps the acceptance of death, or an outcry against it. To look at a photograph is to be reminded of death. One's own and that of others. It can't be helped.

Dear Pia Arke. You know more about these things than me. And yet I think this: that to photograph elements of reality is to imbue them with meaning that is surely unclear to the beholder. I ask myself what you're trying to say with these images, but I receive no reply. For obvious reasons, I can't ask you. You are as silent as your pictures. And your juxtaposing of widely different subjects is puzzling. A right hand, a left. A stuffed toy. A pile of old books. Surgery scars. An illustration depicting dancing pagans. I could analyse my way towards a meaning, following the rational pathways of thought, but the dreamlike quality of monochrome photography would seem to resist such common-sense procedure. Perhaps the woman whose face and closed eyes bring to mind a death mask is dreaming these things? Is it you, the artist, trying to tell me something? Something about yourself? About the history of Greenland? About Hans Egede and his *Perlustration*, in which he lays out his experience of the Greenlanders? I try to grasp what it is, at the same time as I shrink from trying to guess your intentions. Writing about a work of art is reductive.

I must tell you that I know the woman in that photograph. The woman whose breast has been removed. I don't know who she is. I don't mean that woman literally. But the selfsame gaze, the selfsame line of her mouth. I think of it as a Greenlandic gaze, a Greenlandic expression. A resigned, angst-filled look. An expression that passes on her awareness of her own mortality to me. Where is she now, I wonder. In the same place as you?

And that scar. As if she were the victim of a cruel joke. Her numbed flesh has been cut into, an important part of her removed as she slept, and when she awoke the pain had migrated upwards into her gaze. And from there to the beholder. Something that used to be there is gone. Harmony and balance have become disharmony and imbalance. She looks at me: you too will die.

Let's say her name is Orpa. This was in a small, outlying community in East Greenland. She was twenty-three years old. She was going to die, and she knew it. Everything went steadily downhill. She kept being sick and quickly lost weight. Thinner and thinner she became, until her scaly yellow skin revealed the precise contours of her bones. Her beautiful mouth lost its fullness, the skin drew back and her teeth gleamed dully through paper-thin lips. She couldn't eat a thing. I put a tube into her and fed her with nutrition formula, small amounts every hour so as not to overload her stomach, as with a premature infant. But she asked me to stop: it made her nauseous and she couldn't see the sense in receiving nutrients when all it did was prolong her suffering.

I removed the tube. She would still sip sweet tea, and ice-cold water from the lake above the village, which was fed by a melting glacier. But she refused to eat. I asked her permission to administer IV therapy: at least then she wouldn't die of thirst. She agreed. She asked me to give her morphine. 'Why, are you in pain?' I asked. 'Yes, unbearable pain.' So I gave her morphine. And she died. It doesn't take much when a person is teetering on the edge. The last three nights, I slept on a mattress on her floor. She was gripped by terrible attacks, grand mal seizures, presumably due to metastases in the brain. Afterwards, she would lie smiling, as if enraptured.

'Why?' her husband would ask, and tear at his hair. 'Where is the meaning?' Not without humour, Orpa would lift a hand weakly in reply, then lower it again. As if to say: 'How am I supposed to know?' The children looked on with fatigue in their eyes. They were beautiful children. As beautiful as their mother. The same darkly shimmering eyes. Orpa had worked in the supermarket, and her beauty had infatuated me. Every day, I would look forward to going there and buying my groceries. Her

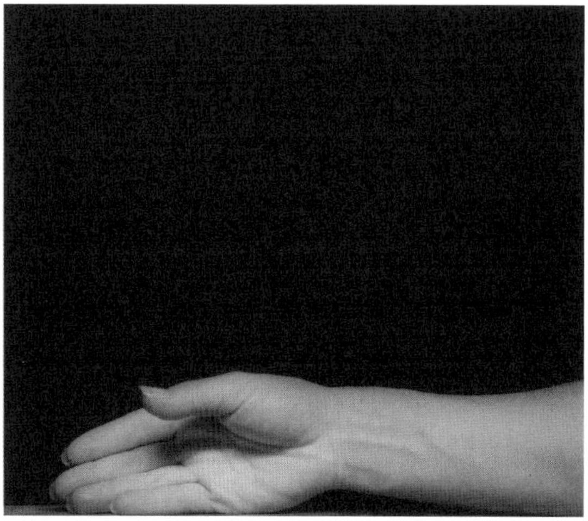

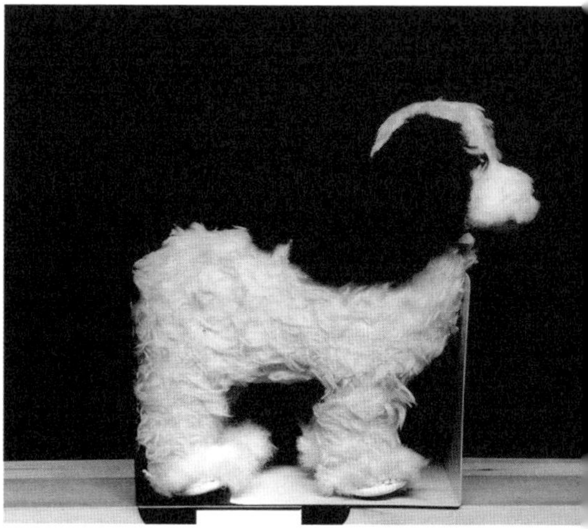

Nature Morte alias *Perlustrations 1-10*, 1994 (continues on the next spreads)

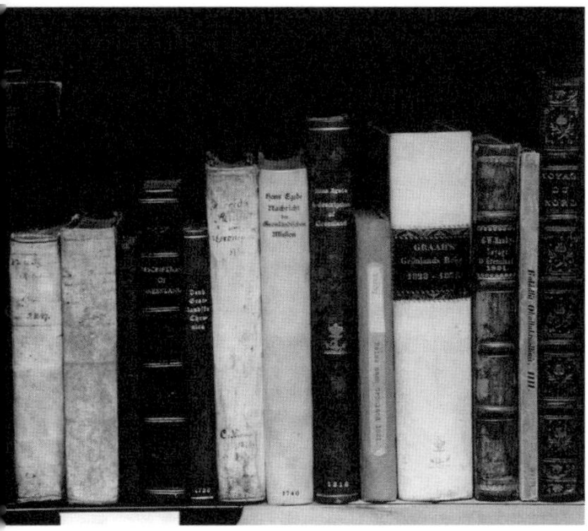
Hans Egede
Nachricht
GRAAH'S
1740

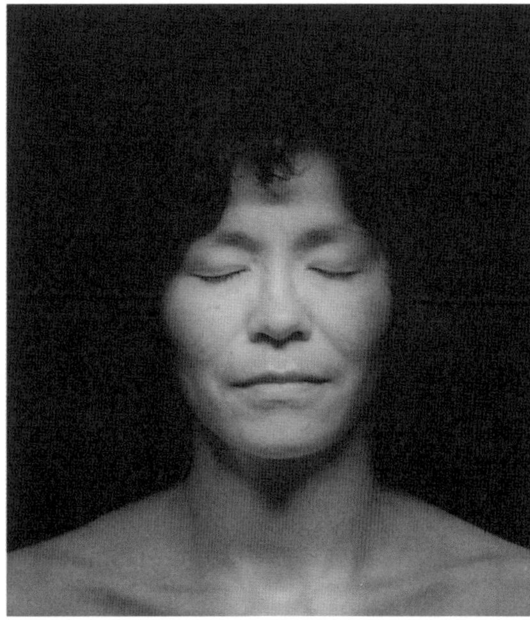

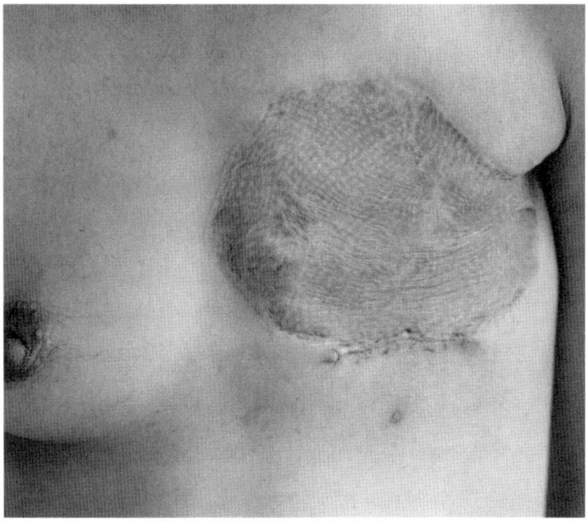

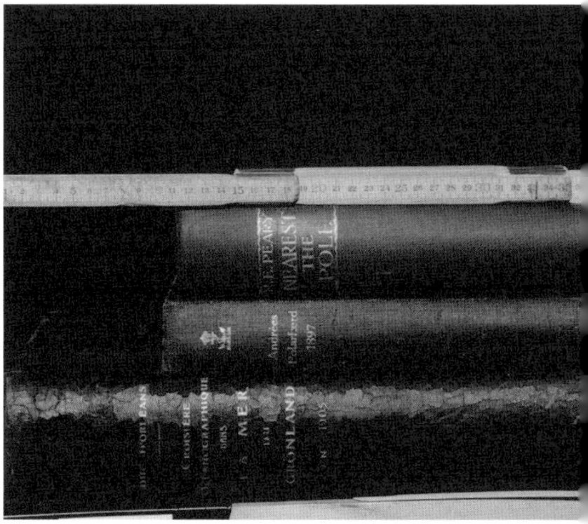

Nature Morte alias *Perlustrations 1-10*, 1994 (continues on the next spread)

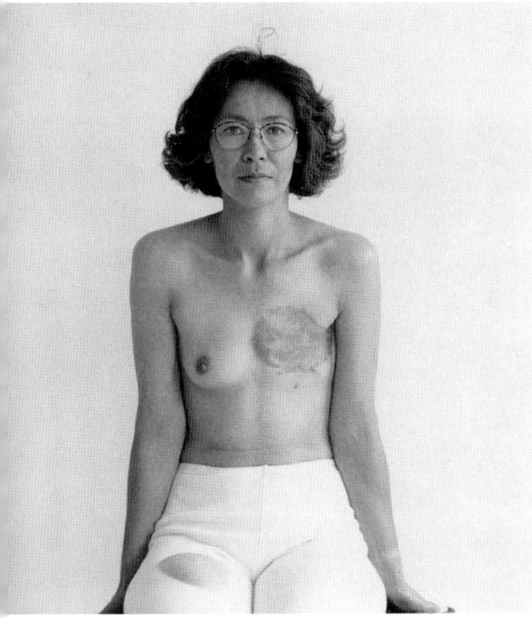

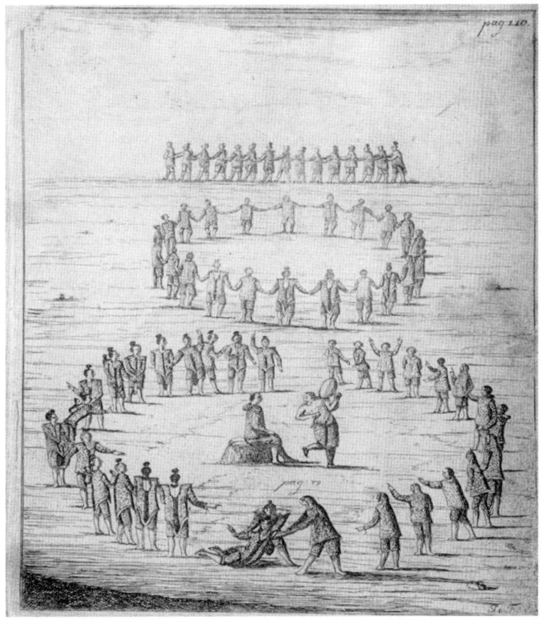
pag 110.

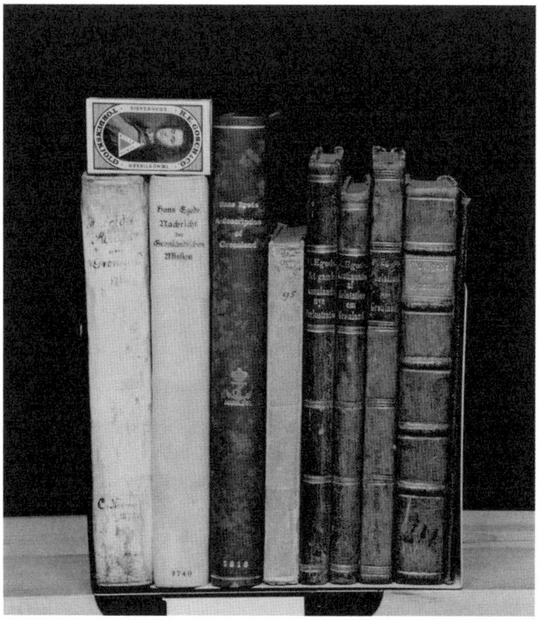

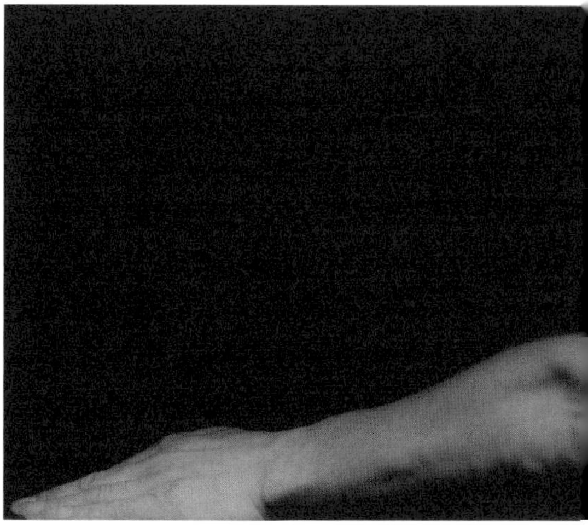

Nature Morte alias *Perlustrations 1-10*, 1994 (continued from the previous spreads)

mother, and her father, the local government legal officer, were silent and took it all with fatalistic composure. It was her husband who cried. He protested. He raged. But he didn't know who to rage against. To be in thrall to undirected rage is very unpleasant. I can quite understand why he began to drink.

Harrowing scenes. But this was the stuff of daily life there. People preferred to die at home. And I dealt with that. I even think I was good at it sometimes. Working as a nurse in such an isolated community, abnormal soon became the norm. Bedding down in a sleeping bag on the floor, for instance, while a beautiful young woman I'd been infatuated with slowly died of cancer. I could deal with that. But I didn't know how to come back from it. Back to what everyone else calls normal. Because it seems anything but normal, once you've got used to that other reality.

It's said that indigenous tribal peoples are afraid of being photographed. However, the huge amount of ethnographic photo resources in the archives of the Arctic Institute, not to mention National Geographic, appears to suggest otherwise. Or perhaps indicates that ethnographers have failed to respect the misgivings of indigenous people about having blankly staring photographic lenses directed at their uncovered skin. Every person is indigenous. Every photographer an intruder. Photographing someone is always to intrude on their personal space. It is to cut a sliver of their life and to deprive it of the truth that is shaped by what went before and what is to come.

Life is horizontal. A photograph is vertical. A surgical intervention. An X-Ray image held up to a light box. A photograph is an irreplaceable loss, as every moment in a human life is a loss. Yet it is a loss we can carry with us, fixed on a sheet of paper. The woman stares at me. I stare at her. But we can never meet. We exist in separate dimensions.

Therefore, the photograph is at once both true and false. The photograph is a paradox. A moment brought to a halt, yet carrying on into eternity. Movement and standstill. Reality and dream. A photograph claims: "This moment exists." Only it doesn't. It's gone.

Nature morte.

Still life.

A story is the opposite of a photograph. Whereas the photograph represents a *moment* in time, the story exploits *time itself.* In writing a story I seek to discover meaning with the help of actions proceeding in time. Time is my developing tray. A student of writing said: 'I'm not interested in narratives.' I'd like to say to her: 'Maybe you should become a photographer instead.'

Perhaps that's why I'm at such a loss trying to describe your pictures. I'm trying to describe a form of expression with the help of another form of expression. Like drawing a sonata. Or singing a ballet.

But that's not the only problem. I'm assuming that you want to convey something to me, to tell me something. Something that's important to you. My antennas are switched on and turned in your direction, my subconscious is primed, my sensitivity to visual impressions, my memory, my capacity to think are all set and ready for me to perform the task I've been given, which is to express your photographs in language, to write about them. But my experience is not your experience; my dreams, my background, my reality are different from yours. Have I even the right to say anything about your pictures? Now that you're dead, you don't have to fret about the current controversy concerning whether or not a writer is allowed to write about experiences that are not their own. You don't have to relate to concepts like "identity politics", "the culture of offence" and "cultural appropriation".

But any encounter between a work of art and its beholder is a collision of separate worlds. The mind moves into alien spaces. The work as such doesn't exist, but is always fluid. It emerges at the point of intersection, in its collision with the mind of the beholder, yet belongs to neither beholder nor artist – or belongs to each on their own. The work is something they construct together, though it is alien to them both. Subsequently, the artist and the beholder go their separate ways, perhaps never to meet again.

It's a very private encounter. It doesn't really concern anyone else. And therefore a work of art is not one work, but many thousands.

Pia Arke. 1958–2007. I don't know you. And you don't know me. The reason is partly that you died the same year my first novel was published. But also that I hardly ever engage with the visual arts. I can confide to you, if you promise not to tell anyone, that modern art feels alienating to me. I think this is the first time I've seen your pictures. I'm on foreign ground. I'm incompetent. I feel undressed.

And as I write these words I see the camera turn towards me, you behind it, adjusting the aperture and focus, the dead eye of the lens staring at me, the shutter opening and closing, and I sense my absolute exposure and become, at the same moment, another of your still lives.

Translated by Martin Aitken

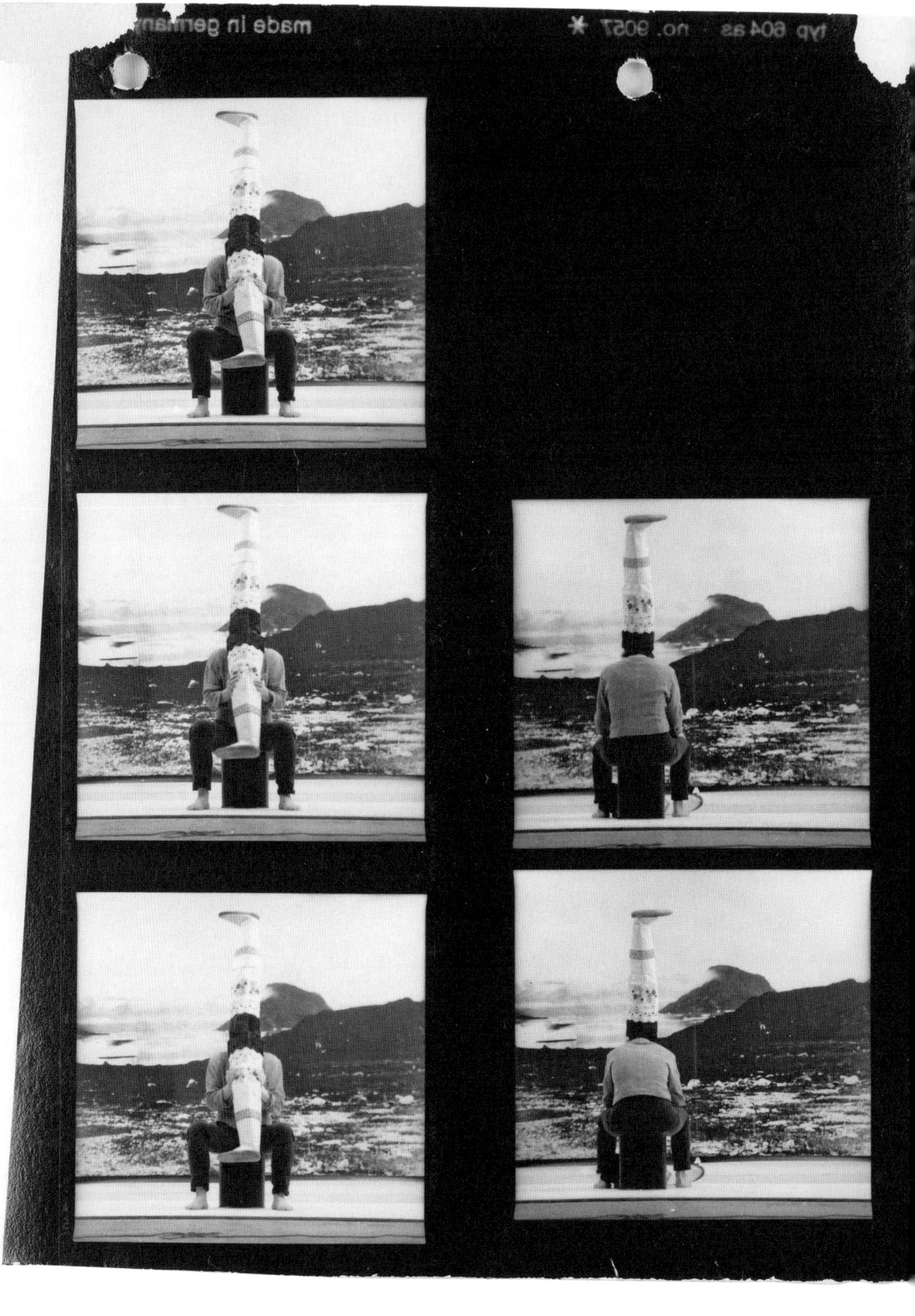

VI

Which Art is Ours?

Interview with Jessie Kleemann

Helle Fagralid

Untitled (Put Your Kamik on Your Head so Everyone Can See Where You Come From), c. 1993

Helle Fagralid: *Would you like to start by telling us about your relationship to Pia Arke?*

Jessie Kleemann: I met Pia Arke in 1986, before she was accepted at the Royal Danish Academy of Fine Arts in Copenhagen. She was in Nuuk, and was a croquis model at the art school where I was principal. There's always a few who are ahead of their time, who have the intellectual capacity to put contemporary currents in a framework and articulate them. Pia saw something before anyone else.

She's probably influenced me much more than I actually realise. After her death I was asked to do a performance in connection with Kuratorisk Aktion's retrospective at Den Frie Centre of Contemporary Art in 2010. I was in doubt about whether I should do it or not. I had so much respect for her. I was also really grief-stricken and maybe I felt a bit inferior to her, so nothing ever came of it.

In my later performances I've realised she created a language for the colonial I also use myself. From there I could make a performance dedicated to one of her works I call *Homage to Soil for Scoresbysund* (2015).

Every time I see her works I'm struck by what an amazingly huge gift it is to be part of that. There's something about the way she incorporates the intellectual in the bodily. I get completely starstruck when I see her art – am both moved and proud. I wonder whether she ever knew how important she already was back then? She probably didn't.

Do you see Pia Arke as a pioneer in the way she works with Greenlandic-Danish colonial history in her art?

Yes. I can't think of anyone else. She was critical of Danish colonisation at an early stage, including in her text for the exhibition *The Flying Kayak* (1993), which she wrote a couple of years before *Ethno-Aesthetics* (1995). She put what a lot of us felt into words: that the colonial gaze still has an impact on us. And she articulated the question of who gets to decide who I am with acute existential precision. I found it astounding that she dared to say that in relationship to Danishness, to Denmark – our 'colonial mother'. But it *had* to be said. As did her criticism of art history – she turned art history upside down.

We're long way from what people used to call 'Eskimo' art. There's a difference between art and ethnographica, such as amulets and tupilak figures made as gifts or connected to rituals. I also think her oeuvre questions whether we should keep making ourselves 'exotic'. She insists that we're something other than that, that we're artists because of who we are, not where we come from. That in itself is a form of investigation, an exercise in reaching a new place.

Do you see her investigative approach and personal point of departure as a way for Pia Arke to choose her own position on the art-history map?

Yes – looking for a deeper level of awareness than something that's been imposed on you. An example: Danish is not my language, but it becomes my language because I speak and internalise it. It used to be like hieroglyphs that I understood visually, because we were taught them in school. But when it becomes part of you, when you adopt the language, then it becomes your own. So when Pia Arke talks about her starting point being personal, she means everything we carry in us as experiences, as bodies. That's what she does with the pinhole camera she took around with her. Or when she wrote *Stories from Scoresbysund*, moving from the big history to the small story, her own family history. I see it as a performance. That's where I think she's influenced many Greenlandic artists.

It's a way for us to start understanding our own art. What art actually is. How art can influence us, can change something.

She inspires and moves me deeply. Not many people have been able to show us that we're enough in and of ourselves – that we don't need outside approval. Art frees me to be who I am. I don't have to go around apologising for looking different in Denmark, or for having different coloured eyes to my siblings in Greenland.

Pia Arke had a Greenlandic mother and a Danish father, and has written about the feeling of being neither/nor or both/and. In her essay Ethno-Aesthetics *she says the feeling of not belonging creates the need for a 'third place'. Could art be that 'third place'?*

I grew up feeling wrong and not belonging, even though both my parents are Greenlanders. Maybe that's why she calls it the 'third place'. Because it's hard to be both. But that's not an issue that's unique to Greenland, it's universal.

Art can blow old frameworks apart, demolish the boxes we get put into. The 'third place' tears down walls. Pia Arke talks about making colonial history personal. That's the source of her art – that whole journey from family photo albums and archives, via Peary and the Explorers' Club in the US, to cartography. There's an 'I' that becomes a you or me. She creates space for human nature. It goes beyond herself. The personal becomes an expansive exercise.

When I enter the space of a performance, feelings beyond my control emerge. I'm open at another level. What she says in *Ethno-Aesthetics* is that there's something we need to open up to. We have to be the subject not the object of art.

Ethno-Aesthetics is about insisting that art can't be defined from a single perspective – a Western European perspective. Pia Arke asks which art is ours, and where it comes from. We have, after all, absorbed Danish and Northern European culture with our mother's milk. It exists, and it's part of us. Maybe that's why so many Greenlanders find it relatively easy to move to Denmark and hold onto their Greenlandic culture. Even though people can still feel split between the two.

Yet it seems as if Pia Arke was able to embrace both worlds, navigate both?

Totally. At the same time as questioning both worlds. In a humorous way too. Maybe people forget the humour, but I think that's where her personality shows. I also think she had fun. In a work like *Untitled (Put Your Kamik on Your Head, so Everyone Can See, Where You Come From)* (p. 58), for example. There's so much humour in her images! It can be difficult to explain, because what you're laughing at is visual. Something I can probably identify as a Greenlander. There's a sense of recognition, an implicit understanding that's not necessarily overly serious. Obviously, when you look at her works and the contexts they appear in, for example the collaboration she had with Stefan Jonsson, then they have a meaning in terms of postcolonialism that's broader and more serious than I think it was in her own 'space', where her approach was often intuitively humorous. As I see it, her humour comes from a loving place. She balances seriousness and the comical with so much to give that makes it possible to laugh at history and the absurdity of the ways it's been told.

The collage Untitled (The Three Graces Collage) *(1994) (p. 31) is compiled of three almost identical photographs of Pia Arke, her cousin Karola Arke Jørgensen, and her childhood friend Susanne Mortensen in front of a photostat of the landscape around Nuugaarsuk. The title is a reference to a famous motif in Western art history based on classical mythology, where the three Graces symbolise fertility, joyfulness and elegance. What do you see in that work?*

The three women are connected, looking at us sternly. I see them as protecting the landscape. Something they can only do with their bodies, their presence, as if to say: "It's ours too." It's not only the people who've drawn the maps and drawn up Arctic conventions that get to define what it is. It's also our bodies, the living part of us.

In another work, also called *The Three Graces* (1993) (pp. 64-65) they're holding different ethnographical objects, something I see as a critical commentary on the art-historical hunt for 'the ethnic' in art, something Pia Arke also talks about in *Ethno-Aesthetics*. It's a conversation she starts by indirectly asking: "OK, so is this how we should stand to make it Greenlandic art?" and "Is Greenlandic art really Greenlandic?". She questions those prejudices. Here too she has a keen eye on how to use humour to highlight the elevated status ethnographica has been given, in both a Greenlandic and Danish context.

I like the fact that they have their backs to us. You're a theatre person like me, and in theatre you only turn your back on the audience to make a really strong point, otherwise it's rare. Here it's as if the three bodies are saying: "It's our turn to tell the story", as they turn towards the landscape – turn their back on any outside gaze.

Next spread: *The Three Graces*, 1993

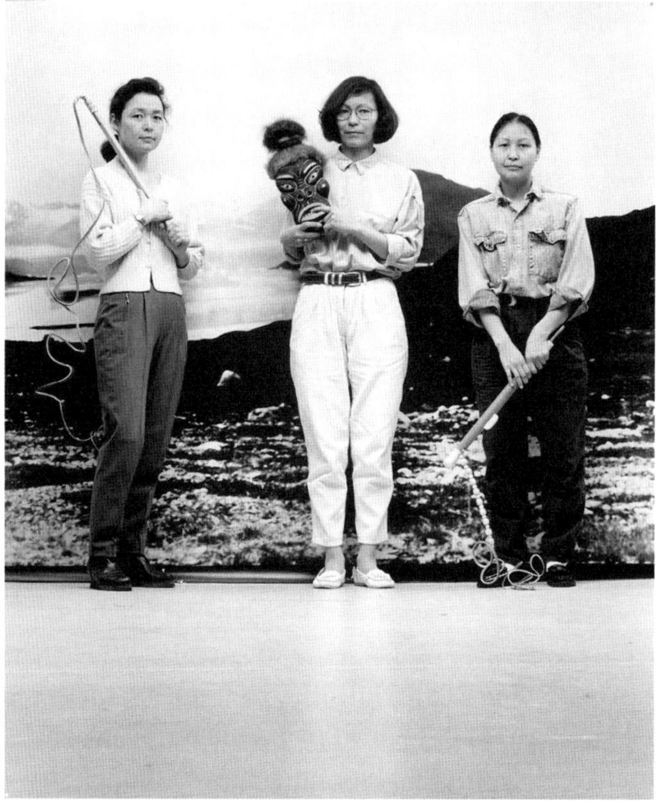

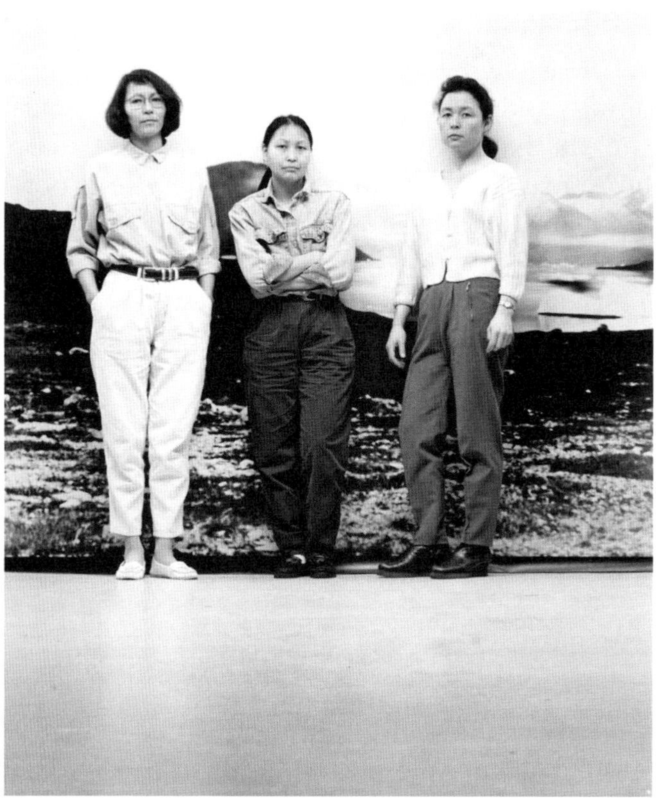

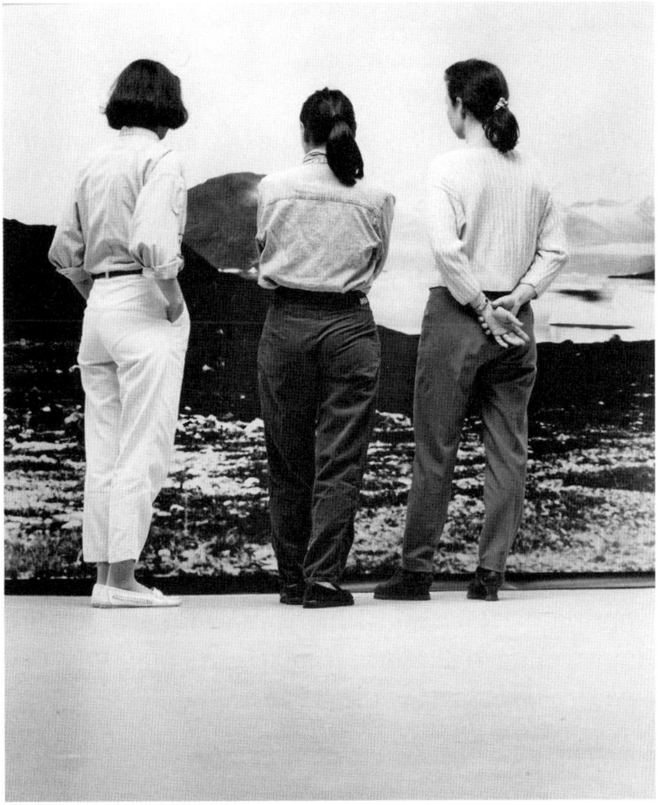

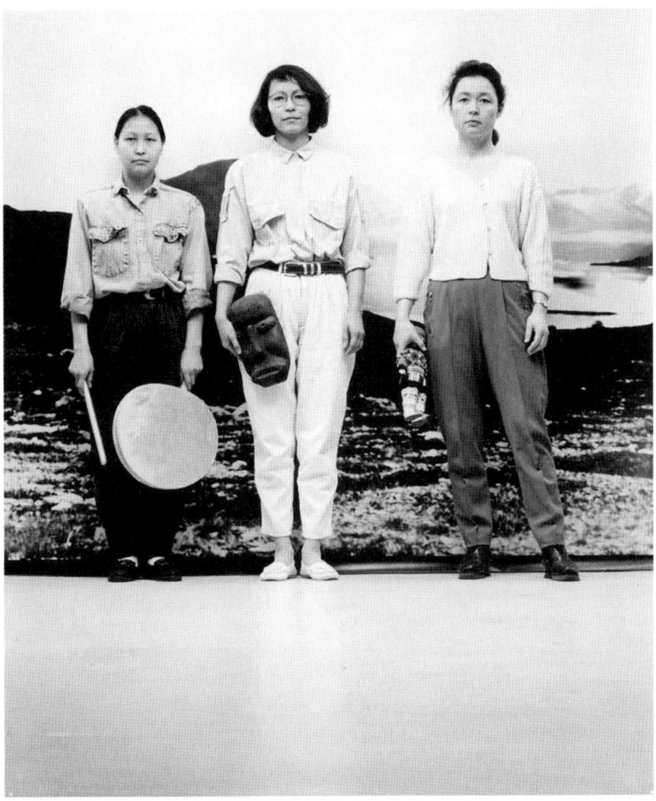

You use ethnographical objects like the Greenlandic frame drum in your own art practice. Are such symbols of culture locked between a Western view of them as a symbol of indigenous Greenlandic culture, and some Greenlanders' view of what it's permissible to do with them today?

There's resistance in Greenland, because some people think it dilutes our culture. Yes, I use the drum in my performances, present my broken drum. I don't play it, I penetrate it with my arm …

It's also about creating a field of tension. Pia created a field of tension. I'm not sure whether we should call it brave – perhaps it was more a necessity. She put herself in a position where it was necessary for her to be critical. It's important to question things, even with people you apparently agree with – and to dare to disagree. It can create something new – create new spaces.

Translated by Jane Rowley

Untitled (Toying with National Costume), c. 1993

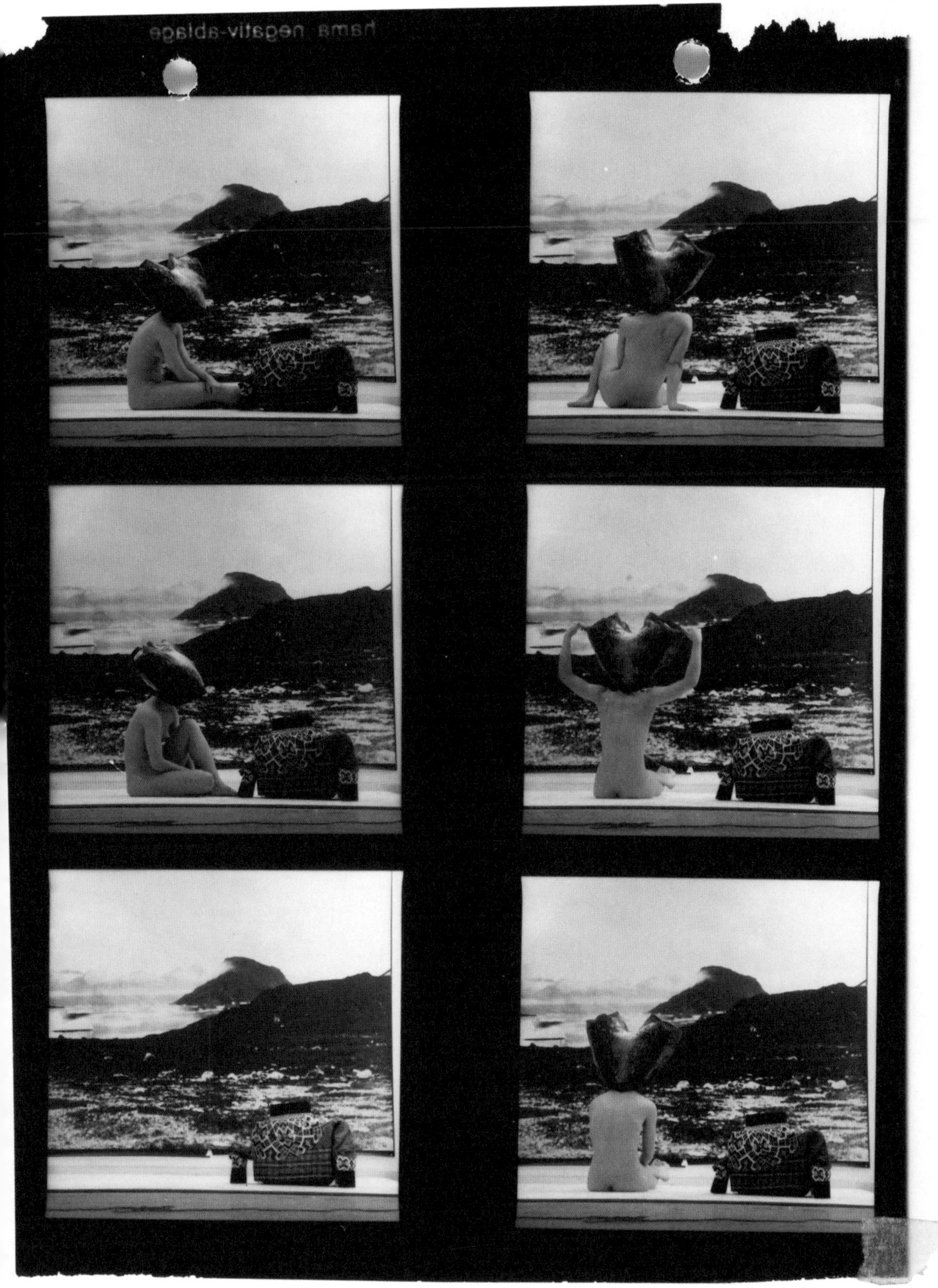
hama negativ-ablage

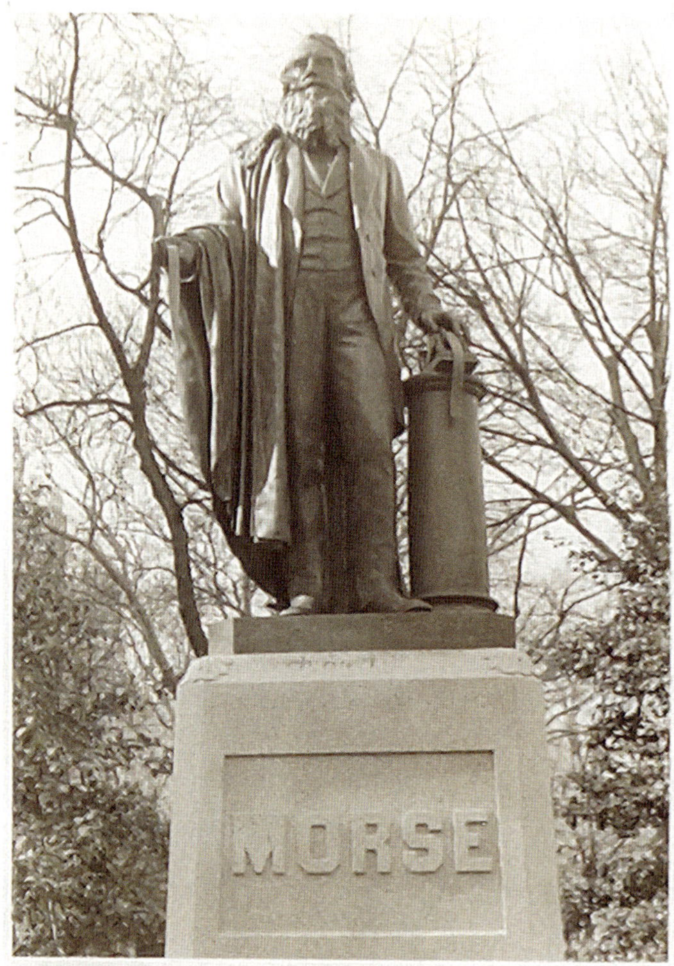

Telegraphy, 1996 (detail)

VII

Work and Reality

Erik Gant

Erik Gant has published several articles about the art of his sister, Pia Arke, including the text for the exhibition *Telegraphy* at the library Kunstbiblioteket Tranen in Hellerup, 1996, which we feature here. To the present publication Erik Gant has added the following accompanying words:

As I remember it, one day 25 years ago, Pia wanted a 'pamphlet' quickly. It has been called a thankless genre, I have later learned – a thistle that grows on poor soils, a message that slanders with fond phrases. We must somehow have had that in mind. We liked to wallow in the idea of ourselves as bastards for whom mother tongue and fatherland were enveloped in mystery.

Heaven and Hell *was included in the text for several reasons. For me all that stuff about identity was an infernal machine, because the identical must always be described in terms of something else. Pia went to work quite differently; for her other people were Heaven. And we met in the context of being exemplary deviants, at the leading edge of all talk of taking possession.*

In the years 1829-32 Samuel F.B. Morse sat in the art galleries of Rome, Florence and Paris and – commissioned by American acquaintances – painted facsimiles of masterpieces of the old world. These oil on canvas facsimiles were praised for their precision and valued as congenial interpretations of their models. After returning to New York, however, Morse gave up his career in visual art and instead engaged in the activity that was to immortalize his name – the invention and development of telegraphy. Telegraphy was a modern way of combating distance and time, more ethereal and less spiritual, a sober form of precision.

Morse plays a central role in Pia Arke's photo-telegraphic series. She took her own photo of his statue in Central Park, New York. The space beside this, on the opposite side from the axis of the series, is filled by a self-portrait of the creator of the other pictures, a Danish telegraphist in Scoresbysund in East Greenland. Morse said of Louis Daguerre's invention that it gave anyone the chance to be a painter in his own right. Morse's own invention would in addition give the telegraphist the opportunity to realize himself on the one hand as the prophet of the global village and on the other, in his leisure time, as an explorer in his own right. The pictures. arranged in a system of reflections and contrasts, recount his story – a story of sending himself out and sending himself home again, the story of a society in a particular stage of being affected, a telegraphic now-or-never somewhere between the too early and the delayed.

This now-or-never that Pia Arke seeks is her own origin. She is descended on the one hand from shamans recently converted to Christianity, on the other hand from a family of Copenhagen *petit bourgeois* – an incomprehensible origin once one has abandoned it. At all events she insists that photography is part of her origin, and photo-telegraphy, her attempt to send herself home by sending herself out in all possible directions, can be seen as a recurring theme in her works. She grew up with photographic freezing of the remains of an original nature – the enthusiastic photographer's embrace of local beauties, the captivating beauty of the arid surroundings and the beauty in and among the still-so-natural people with their entirely unjustified and infectious joy in life. All these pictures – taken at the last moment and mounted in the family albums of friends or acquaintances or reproduced in popular and scientific publications – are her material.

It is thus usually very clear that the pictures are there to begin with, and that Pia Arke first and foremost exposes them to her own questioning of what she is to do with all these documents, all these minutely detailed registrations. The question is how one *takes* (as one can put it) a picture, which in turn raises the issue of what happened to all those documented and registered last moments. Pia Arke asks these questions and offers attempted answers to them by letting the found picture fade deeply into the blue distance, thus on the one hand giving time more colour to work with, and on the other emphasizing the aestheticization that already plays into the pictures' reproductions of original objects.

Both here in the latest work and in the earlier ones – in the experiments with the "camera house," with the optics, with the traditional art photograph's capturing of nature's own graphics, with the framework of the photograph – in the thematization of the white man's comprehension of and assault on *the original* and *the other* – everywhere the undermining doubt comes to expression and helps to keep Pia Arke's production hovering somewhere between the aesthetic and the authentic, between work and reality. Nevertheless her pictures are not primarily about a desperate search for the precise expression of self and origin. The main thing, as she herself says, is that the photograph *works*, that it creates unlikely connections, that it brings her into contact with (the heaven and hell of) other people.

Translated by James Manley

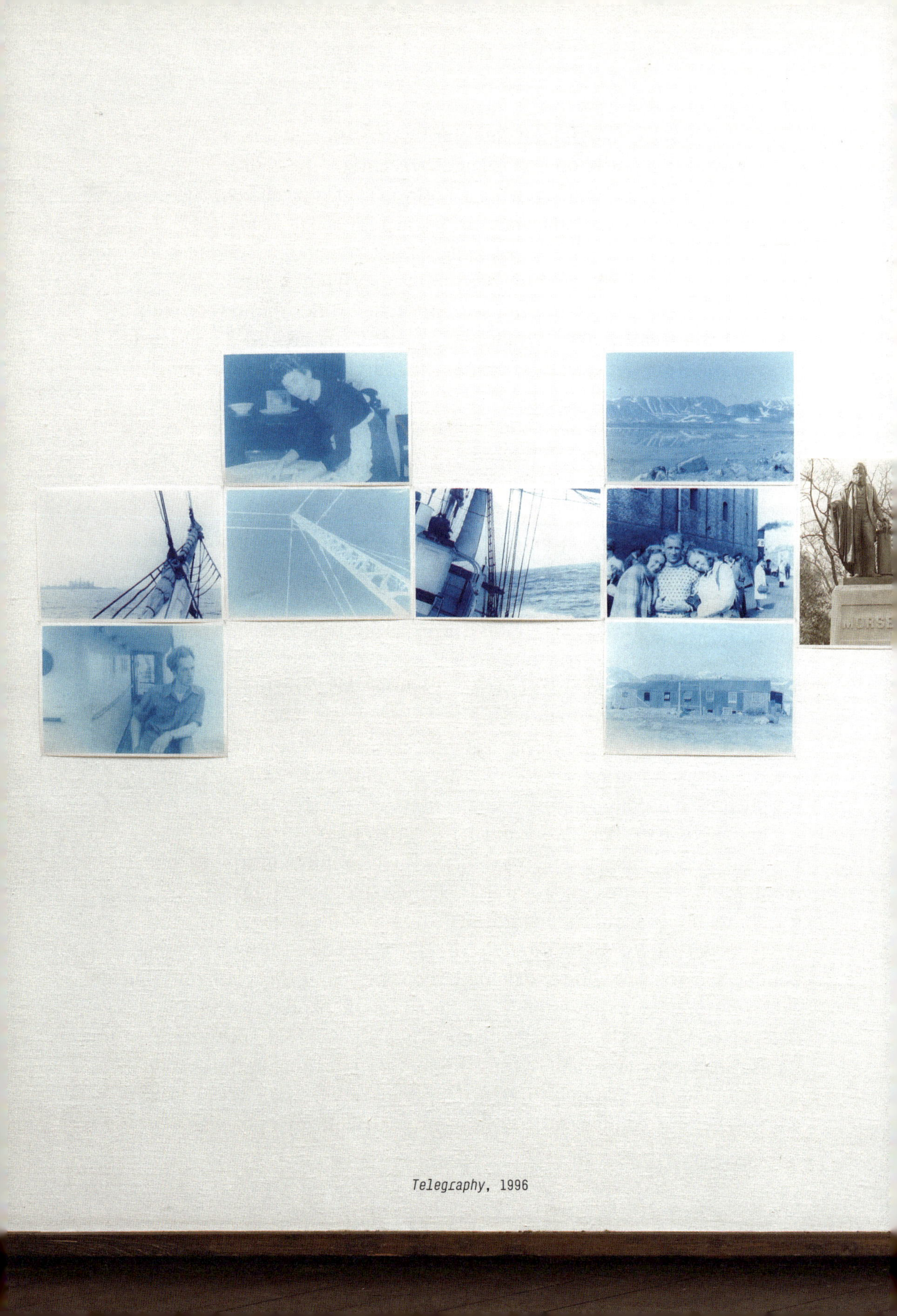

Telegraphy, 1996

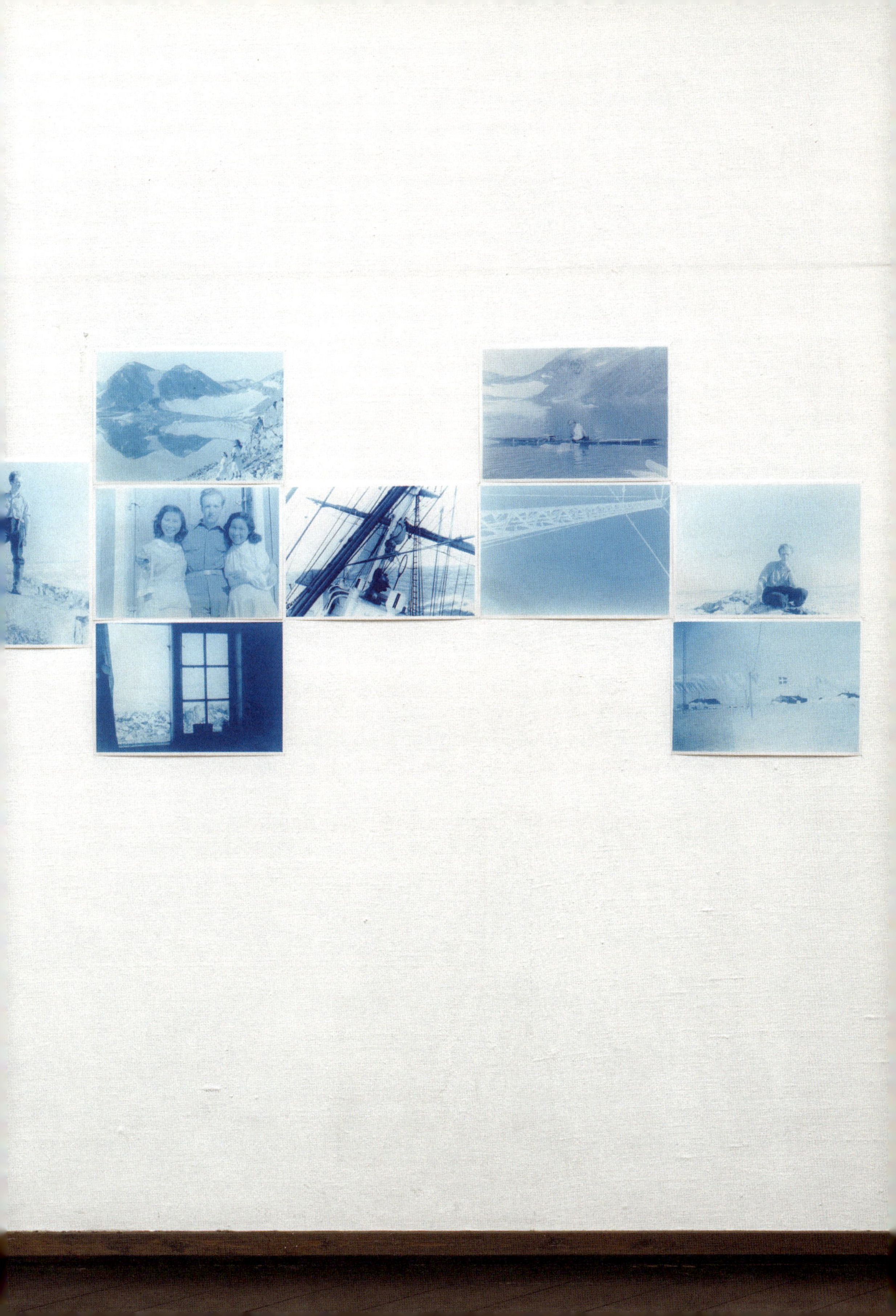

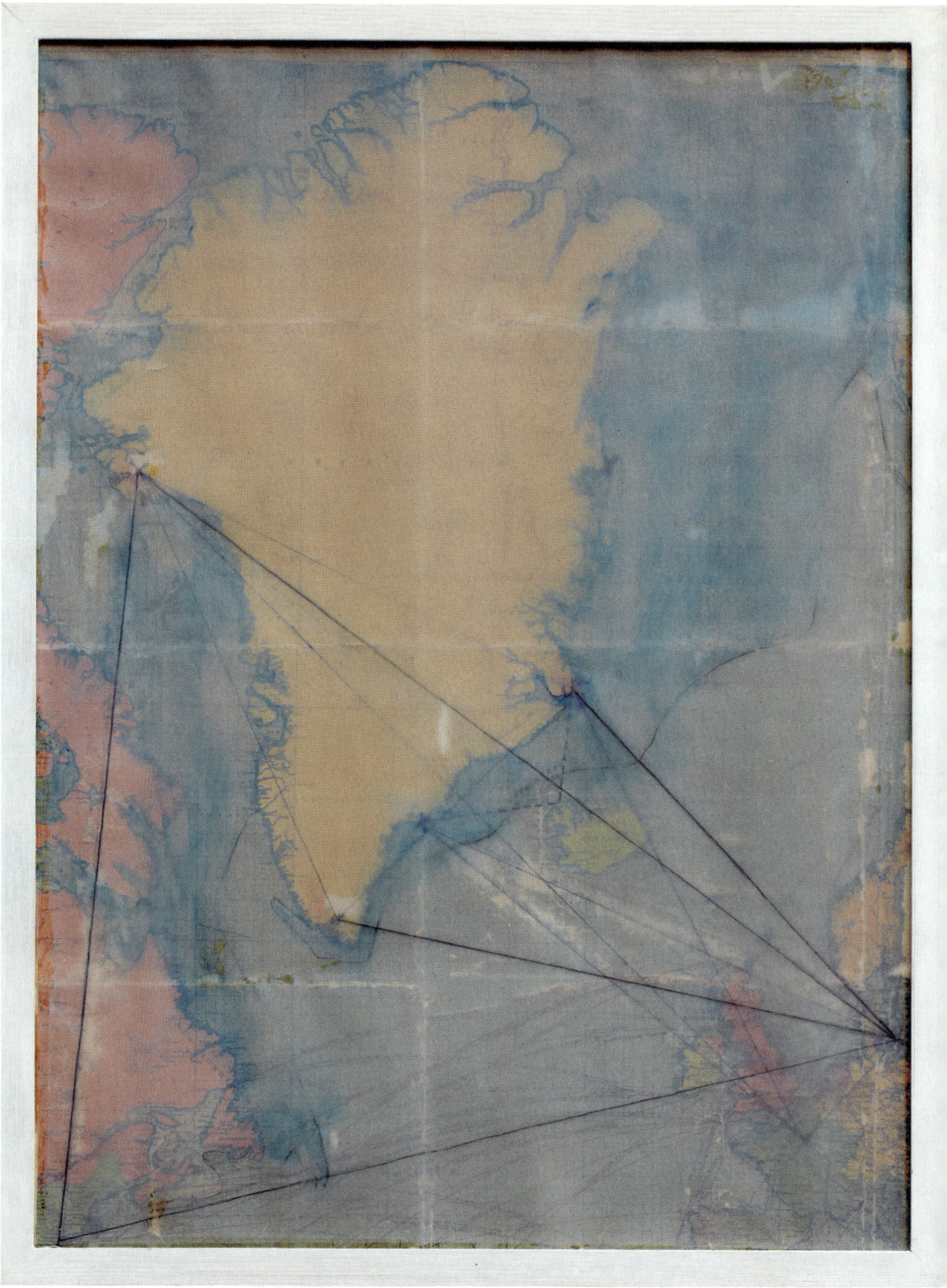

VIII

Interior Viewpoint

Darren Almond

Old School Map, c. 1992

A curator once told me that he didn't feel the need to physically visit places of historical significance or consequence in order to gain an understanding of what took place there: he would be able to attain what was necessary through accounts using the written word. He would simply read in order to understand. If we did this, then I feel we would extinguish the subtle but consequential ripples of historical events before they even had a chance to reach the shoreline of a second generation. The curator's statement horrified and disgusted me at the time – how can you presume to understand anything from the written word alone? So much of what we know is gained from what we can't even see, let alone transcribe into words.

The landscape, and particularly the weather in it – often omitted from discussion – is what illuminates our total understanding of place and sense of reason. For my part, I have found myself many times at the edge of humanity in the far north, beyond the Arctic Circle, trying to grasp what it is to be in the semblance of the Arctic wastelands. Winds raging against me, sub-zero temperatures, nasal passageways frosted shut; in one extreme case my retinal liquid froze, rendering my vision impaired, fixed beyond a point of focus. No moisture in sight, despite being surrounded by ice alone, but squalls of diamond dust in free flight caught by the light of a never-setting sun. Refractions of such clarity and piercing beauty, a labyrinth of the sublime. Such a confusing term, wastelands. A space of limitless scale where the body stands alone, pitted against vast tundra and magnetic storms in the night sky.

In the final section of *The Waste Land*, "What the Thunder Said", T.S. Eliot reflects upon a land without water, where little will grow. In a small digression, the poet infers a hallucination of a third person for our travel companion. This is something which, as Eliot himself noted, was inspired by one of Ernest Shackleton's expeditions, where one of his men suffered from the delusion that there was one more man amongst their group, an imagined but real third person. Another human form in contact with the present and present within the landscape, never 'seen' but belied to history through the image of association alone.

Considering Pia Arke and her pinhole box camera, it is easy to assimilate connections between her camera obscura and its associated histories: Fox Talbot and his 'Mousetrap', the desire to collect some semblance of exactitude of place. However, there is no scientific precision here, no fiducial marker in place. Across these four images (pp. 78-79) a similar landscape is drawn, two recorded perspectives aligned towards one single point. Exposures vary in accordance with time's duration. But the resulting images from Arke's dark chamber seem somehow to address a space that exists off-camera. There is a body present. There's also an invisible weight, for the viewer: of not knowing what lies ahead of or farther beyond the distant mountains. Even within the gestural application of the chemicals needed in order to capture these exposures of time, weather, light and place, there seems to lie the form of a figure, present through its absence. Reductive photography at a primal threshold point of observation. These images are compelling even before the reader discovers the biographical background to their awakening.

Greenland as a landmass alone reaches the farthest north above sea level and is the largest island on the planet. The Arctic is literally the Antarctic's polar opposite, predominantly surrounded by landmass, all with varying political designations, and yet harbours none. The main entrance north for global ocean currents is via the North Atlantic, crossing through the designation of Arke's familial trajectory which sits astride this gateway up to the Arctic Ocean. It's hard to quantify a hidden landscape as vast as Greenland. I have only ever flown over its terrain and gawped at its beauty, breathless in scale. Devoid of any geological markings as seen from above, flying overhead towards the Americas the Great Circle casts its trajectory repeatedly over Greenland's southern regions. Only at its perimeters are there any signs of life.

In coming to Arke's work remotely, I was initially compelled by her triangulation hand-drawn across a large, outlined and annotated educational map (p. 75). School maps have a habit of charting dreams. Arke's movements in the early stages of her life were determined by her father's work in radar communications: these matters of weather and of watching inscribed this triangulation and left an embedded imprint. If Arke sees the map of Greenland as resembling the distorted, monstrous head of Joseph Merrick, I have always seen it as a single severed left lung. Even more so after looking at her *Legend* collages (pp. 93-97), where the intricacies of waterways, fjords and sea channels are outlined and highlighted like the arteries of a respiratory tract. The very ventricles of our existence. There are the two seasons at the far north, the dark and the light. During these, the ice floes form and melt, grow and recede in

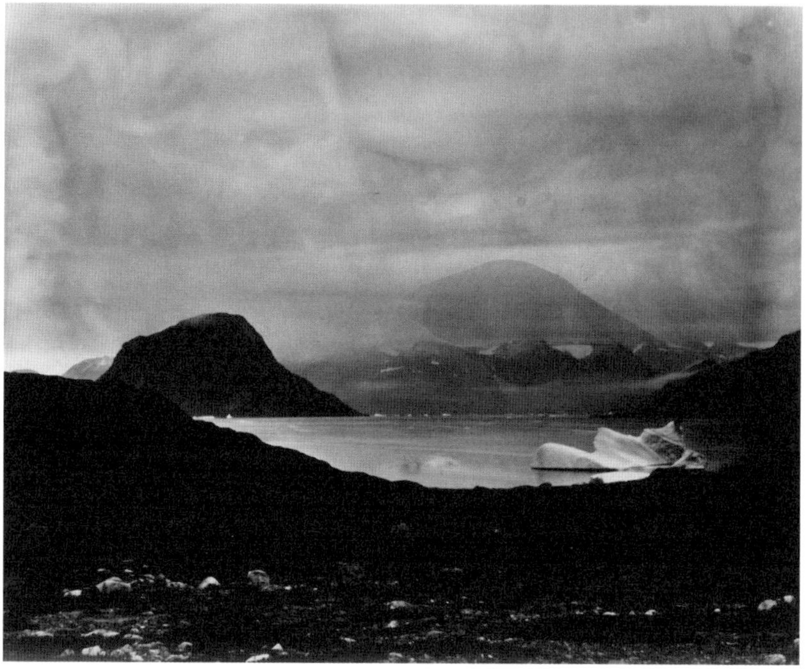

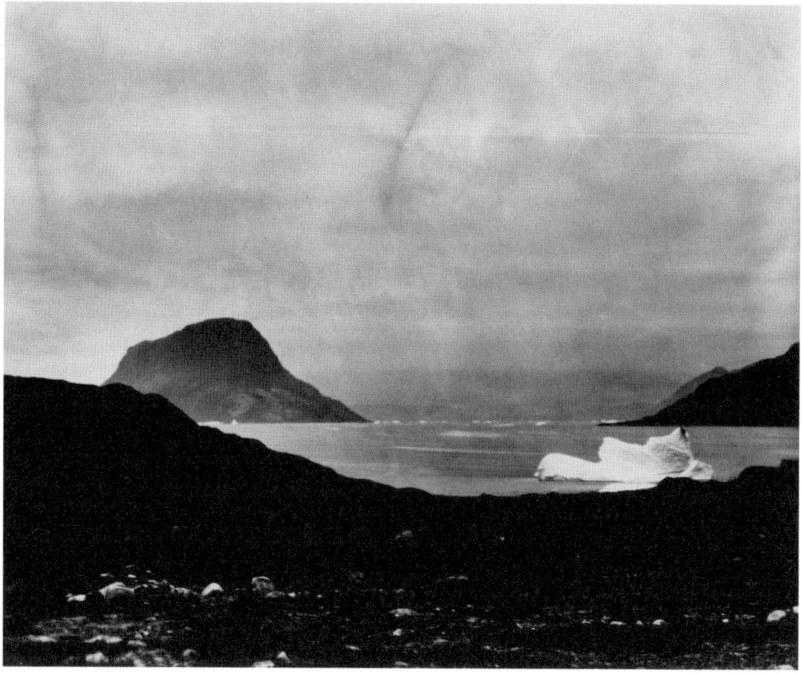

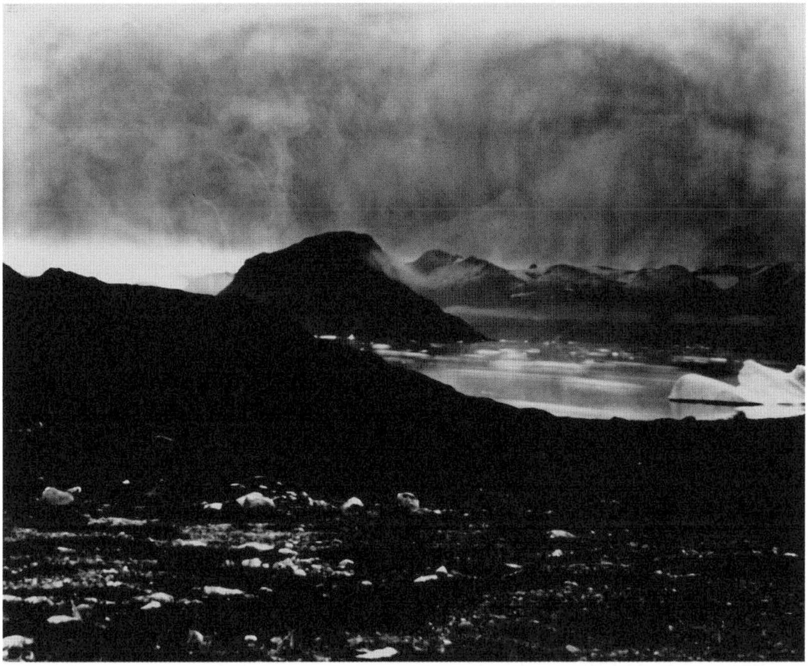

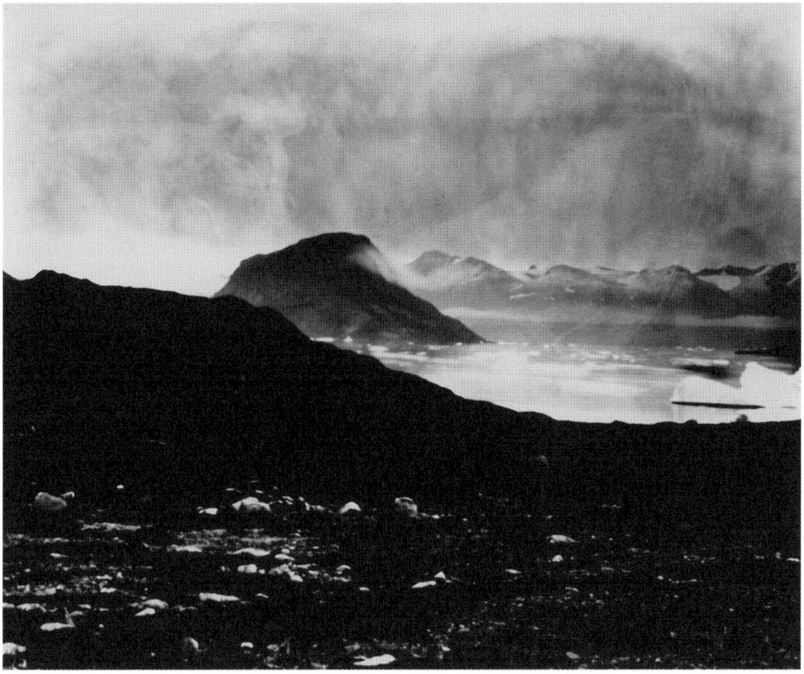

Nuugaarsuk alias *Pinhole Camera Photograph* alias *The Point*, 1990

accordance with current climatic pressures. The landscape breathes and it breathes slowly, inhaling and exhaling with every planetary circumnavigation of the sun. Ice of any nature is always in a state of flux, dictated by the atmosphere which surrounds it.

Pertinent to the images taken at Nuugaarsuk are the climatic conditions. We see in the bay an iceberg, but not one of significant grandeur, and in the distant hills a mild scattering of low-lying snow. We are beyond winter here, we can see the bay has navigable waters, we are away from the endlessness of the long winter's night. And if we apply a modicum of reason we would need to be under some sense of sunlight in order for Arke's magical box to capture a documentation at all. She would need a break in the clouds in order to capture any ghost of an image. But there would be no rush. The resulting images, however, appear at that liminal point in time between dark and light, between daytime and nightfall. The iceberg remains stationary but the ocean levels its swell. The clouds pass by and the exposures would lengthen in time; sat inside the camera would be a sensible place to be, watching as the weather diffuses the artist's landscape of recollections.

A starting point and place of departure. This is how I see these four images combined. There is an enormity of scale beyond those distant hills, which I find intriguing, but getting here was Arke's first major step and in doing so triggered further avenues of a more complex and political nature. She had returned to a place that was lost and needed to be found, and from there, sat in her box, she was able to trigger a dialogue born of necessity and self-awareness. To induce a certain critical meditation on your subject without knowing its ultimate direction is an artist's path. I can fully relate to the waves of process that carry the body forward into unknown landscapes by way of addressing the self and its relations to and from its existence. The actual activity of being 'in place' ignites a question that is the hardest to answer. Dancing with the spirit of yourself within a cube hidden from view, but ultimately on show. The world turns regardless, dictated by the scale of reason, to the time of place and to the place in time.

Far from the visible, there has been a recent discovery. This gigantic island has contained something which, due to Arke's sad and early passing, was kept from her within her lifetime. The impregnable interior of Greenland holds a shadow. A mega-canyon, buried a mile or more beneath the ice and discovered in 2013 by ice-penetrating radar. V-shaped, running north from the Central Region up and into the Arctic Ocean, this is the longest canyon discovered on the Earth to date, beyond 750 kilometres in length and up to 800 metres deep and 10 kilometres wide. In the exhibition we can see the actual photographic negative cell from Arke's pinhole camera, her map-work renderings and the flesh wound documentation of Susanne Mortensen's cancer treatment (p. 85). All of which combine together to expose the body as landmass. Nothing is more explicit than the topographic image captured by NASA; this hidden perspective of Greenland's interior is startlingly similar to that of radiographic scans of cancerous lungs and to Arke's *Legends*. For humanity's sake I hope that this particular geological secret remains hidden far from view.

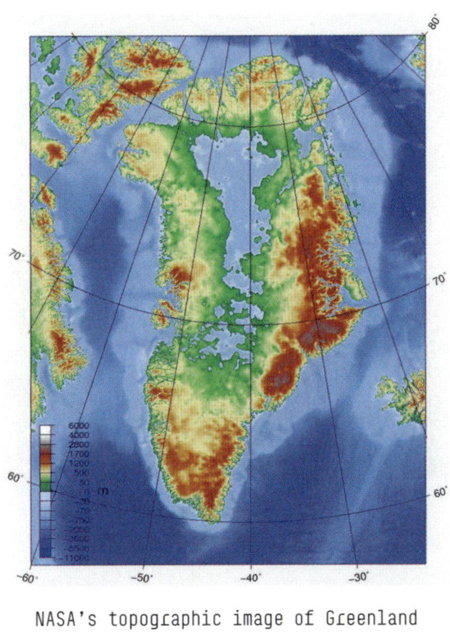

NASA's topographic image of Greenland

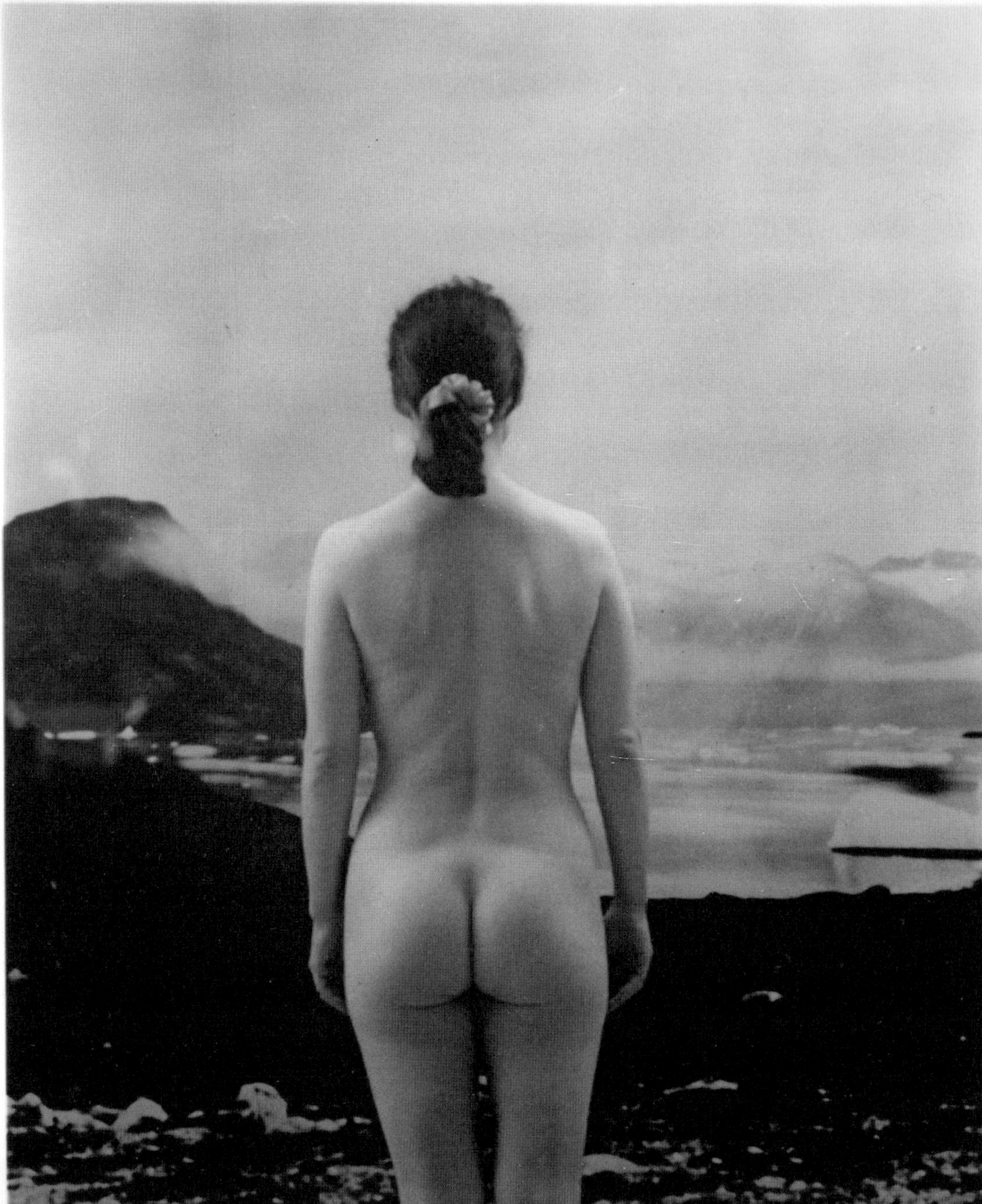

Self-Portrait, 1992

IX

Body and Map:

A Leitmotif for Pia Arke

Anders Kold

Five enormous collages made from maps of Greenland, added photographs, graphite paint and colonial goods, *Legend I-V* (1999) (pp. 93-97) is an indisputable high point of Pia Arke's work. The maps, showing the area around Scoresbysund, are impressive by their sheer scale. Personally, I toggle between being awed by their beauty, which owes much to the blue-and-red cartographic rendering, and the unpleasant feeling of knowing that they are parts of a larger body. The maps' (vivi-)sectioning is understandable enough – these are at once both locations and collages. However, from the fragmentation emerges the shadow of amputation: something has been removed from a greater, natural whole. Last winter, inspecting the works for this exhibition, I photographed a number of details with my phone. Later, when I looked through the pictures, the shadow reappeared as a grim synaptic link between *Legend III* and an image from Arke's other monumental work, *Nature Morte* alias *Perlustrations 1-10* (1994) (pp. 50-54). With cartographic sobriety, Arke records the scar from the removal of her childhood friend Susanne Mortensen's left breast. The likeness to the modified map, to which sugar adds a relief-like effect, is uncanny. A landscape among many others in Arke's work, this image is a reminder that map and body are a leitmotif for the artist.[1]

Starting in 1988, when Arke more or less definitively abandons the medium of painting, the dominant features of her art are tracing, material overlays, photographic superimpositions and bodily contact with the landscape, or images of it. Over the course of a decade, Arke becomes the Danish artist who first and most comprehensively converts the distance and silence of colonial history into a central theme of contemporary art. It is not unusual for an artist, in her work, to point out aspects of life that hurt. Arke certainly did. Personally engaging with history, she revealed her points of pain. Moreover, it is often from the wound, and her consciousness of it, that the hope of healing radiates.

It seems almost prophetic that Arke and her then partner, the Danish artist and printmaker Michael Petersen, used flour to mark out a 10 by 10 metre square flat rock surface outside the capital of Nuuk in summer 1988 (pp. 86-87). Wheat, which is not grown in Greenland, is one of the five colonial goods Arke used to add body to the maps in *Legend I-V* – the others are sugar, rolled oats, coffee and rice. Mapmaking – seizing, surveying and setting down the contours and physical makeup

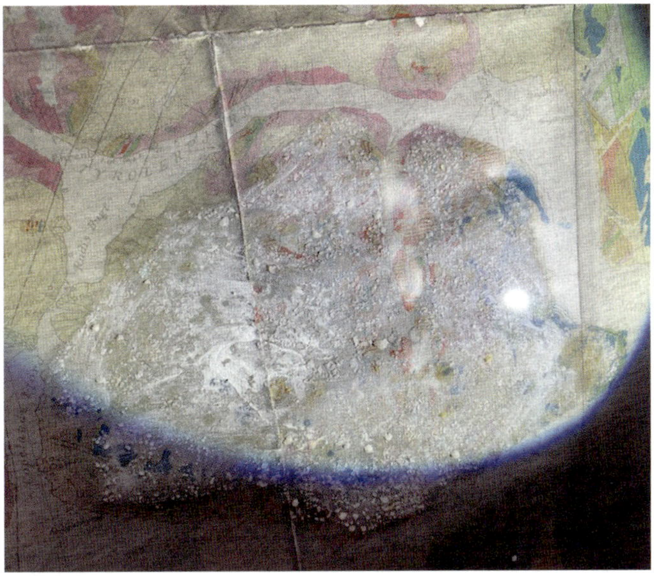

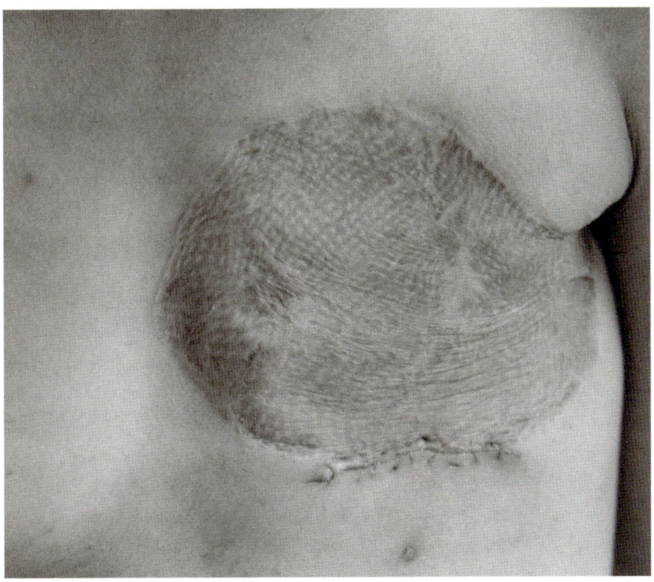

Top: Detail of *Legend III*, 1999
(mobile phone picture)

Bottom: Detail of *Nature Morte* alias *Perlustrations 1-10*, 1994

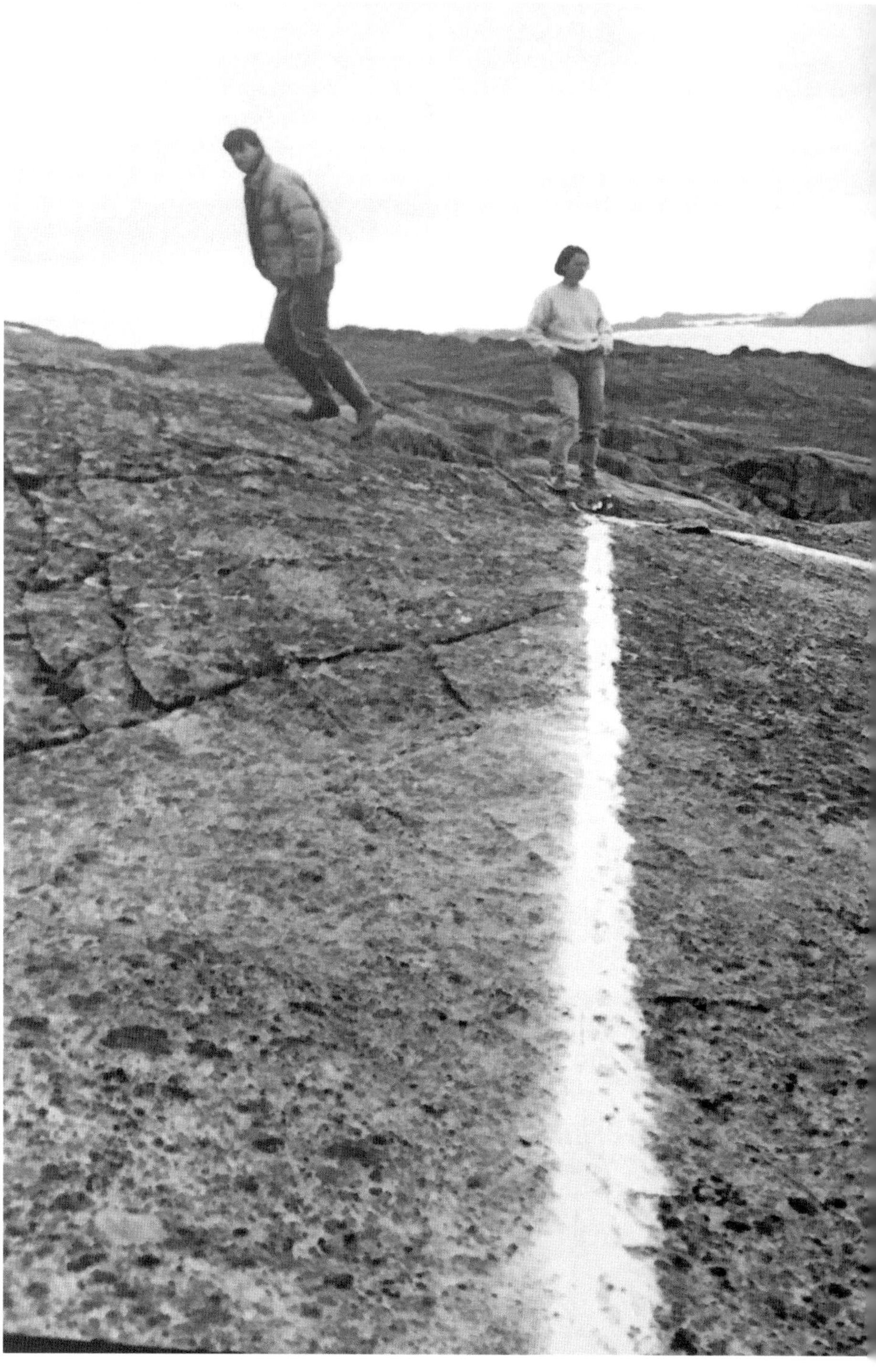

Pia Arke with assistants in Nuuk, 1988

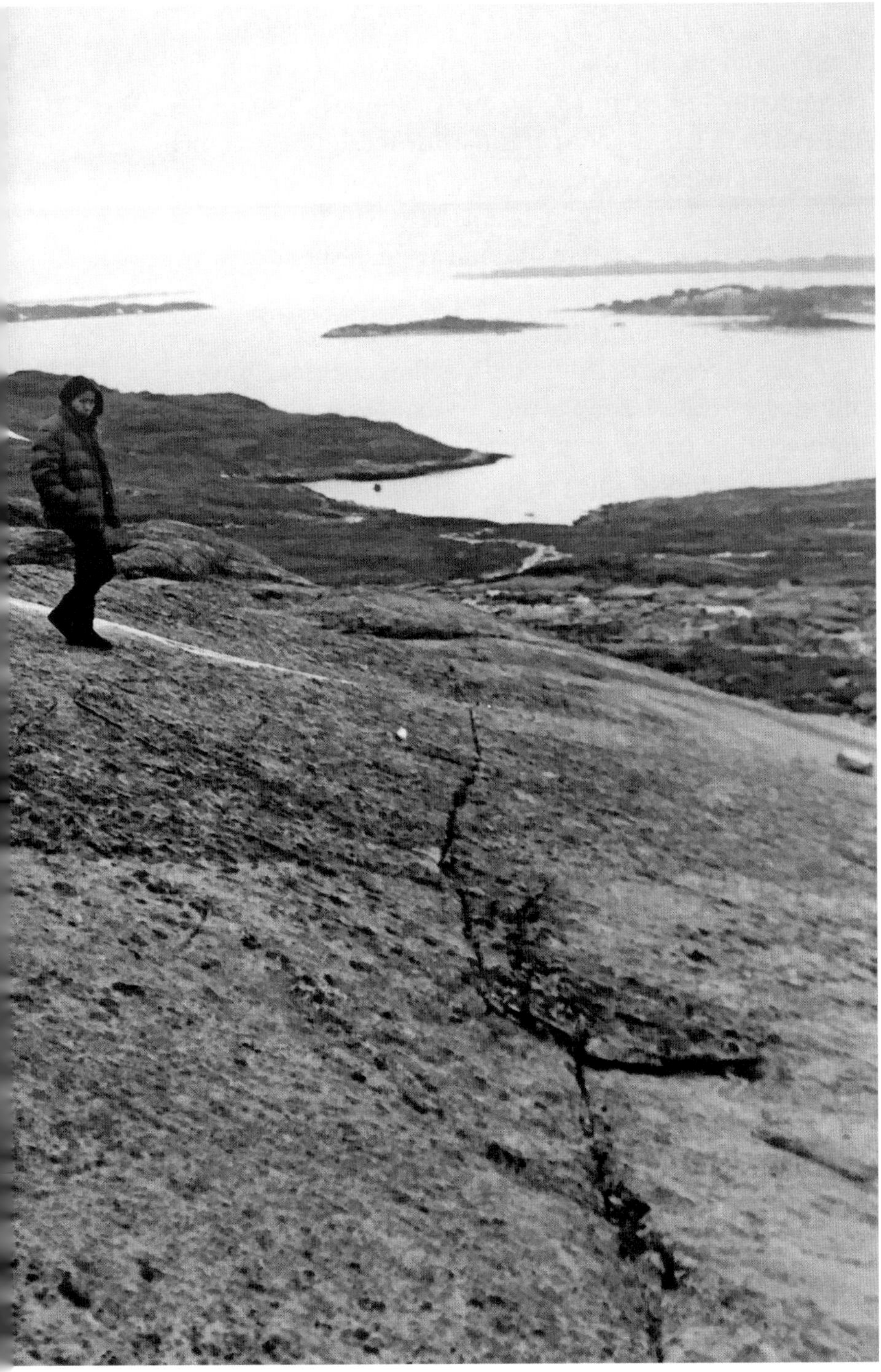

of a landscape in coloured lines on a plane – is obviously an act of superimposition bound up with the history and activity of colonial Denmark in Greenland. The square at Nuuk was subsequently painted in what might be called a late-modern ultramarine recalling the French artist Yves Klein. A photograph shows Arke standing confidently at the vanishing point of two lines. Something begins here, which was also her first physical touchdown as an artist in the landscape she grew up with but later had to leave.

Considering that she was the child of a Danish father and a Greenlandic mother, her sense of belonging to either country always unclear and divided, it is not so strange that Arke's work came to reflect a state of being in motion. In her work, the subject of changeability also offers a promise of the ability to affect change, while indicating difficult issues of identity. There she begins and ends. All along, landscapes are involved, both when she threw her mind into the process from her apartment in Copenhagen and when Greenland was her physical setting.

In 1990, Arke takes a number of pictures with a self-timer, showing herself at a school-like desk in her Copenhagen apartment, acting out a variety of scenarios in double exposures. On the rear wall in one of the

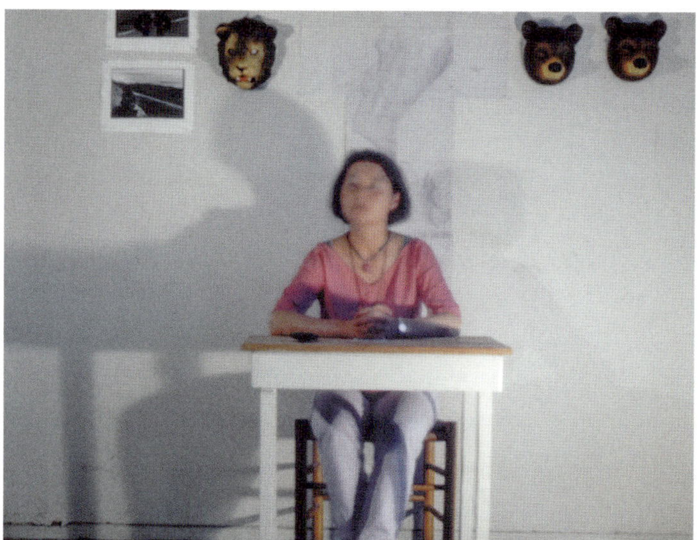

Untitled (Double Exposure Self-Portrait in Interior), 1990

pictures hangs a section of a map of Greenland and two photos from the work on the rock at Nuuk two years before. Early on, the connection between photographic and cartographic representation and the artist's own body is put into play. Shortly after, Arke brought her homemade pinhole camera to Narsaq, using it to capture distant Nuugaarsuk Point: the view from her childhood home (pp. 78-79). While the image of the landscape was being impressed on the light-sensitive film at the back of the box, Arke was moving towards the origin she had been separated from in her teenage years when she was sent off to boarding school in Denmark. In the years that followed, the image of Narsaq becomes a leitmotif for Arke. Over the next decade, it also becomes a tense and emotionally loaded ground and mirror for many other pictures.

A series of self-portraits from 1992 (pp. 20, 42 and 82), which is often used to illustrate Arke's work, is significant to the discussion of the relationship between body and landscape. The artist photographed herself not in Greenland but in front of one of her pictures of Greenland. The work is permeated by a mood of remoteness, as if she were observing Greenland through a pane of glass. The work brings to mind the solitary, back-turned figures of the German Romanticist painter Caspar David Friedrich. We might also entertain the notion that she is intuitively re-performing experiences she might have had at such institutions as Denmark's Natural History Museum before dioramas of the arctic world featuring, perhaps, a back-turned, fur-clad Inuit as a human marker against the blinding whiteness of the landscape.[2] The time Arke embodies in front of the large print is not one of lost origin but a divided, probing, confrontational now. If dioramas seek to freeze time, perennially at risk of representing something that is no more, Arke sets time and, in turn, the world in motion. Arke was hardly a romantic, and the unique feeling of fitting in neither here nor there only grows from this point on, with the image of Narsaq as a leitmotif.

The 1996 film *Arctic Hysteria* (p. 38) is Arke's most famous and, in a way, most radical work in the interface of body and landscape. The artist's feet are first seen, in a bird's-eye view, contemplating a photo on the floor of her apartment. After a forceful zoom into the landscape, she crawls into it naked, her motives inscrutable. Observing, exploring, sniffing the landscape, she starts rolling around and crawling on her belly across it, before tearing the picture into strips, as if to build a nest from it, until, ultimately, she crawls off again. She is in her own space. At no point does she look at the viewer, shielding herself from eyes that might seek to categorize the figure before them. First and foremost, she is a curious, searching body connecting with the landscape – a landscape of/after her own mind, we might say, that she created inside a box she made herself according to the dimensions of her own body.

The large *Legend* works carry histories great and small about places and people who once were. But Arke's art is never sentimental, and far from unequivocal. If, as mentioned, we might shudder at the grim links to some of her other works, there are also constructive and wide open perspectives to be derived. One is that history, which must inevitably be written anew, is full of women with agency (men, meanwhile, make rare appearances in Arke's work and seem stuck in their historical roles). While it may have been men – white men from all over the world – who named everything on the maps, the *Legend* works overlay the maps with images of women. It may seem obvious, but when writing the history of art, it is important also to view Arke in the light of feminism, as a prominent feminist artist. Furthermore, this perspective should not be shaded by overarching decolonial agendas, especially considering that the methods involved essentially feed one another. The images of people affixed to the maps of Scoresbysund not only serve as a band aid, they also introduce the work as a palimpsest, maps and people layered on top of one another with considerable historical depth.

The photos, taken on a trip by the Danish telegraph operator Svend Lund Jensen to Scoresbysund in 1947 – incredibly, capturing the artist's mother, Birgitte Justine Piparajik Arqe – are not only protected by parchment as in old photo albums. Furnished with cartographic signatures on the parchment, they were included in the Danish polar explorer Svend Lauge Koch's report from his expedition to the area in 1931–34, an expedition closely related to Denmark's attempt to convince and eventual success in convincing the World Court in The Hague that all of North East Greenland was Danish territory. The artist's maternal grandmother had been shipped there in 1925 as a pawn in the ongoing territorial dispute between Denmark and Norway. In all, 87 people from 10 families 1000 kilometres south were enlisted to methodically change the history of the land's national affiliation. These are the historical upheavals Arke takes up in her legends about this spot on the big island. Arke's work

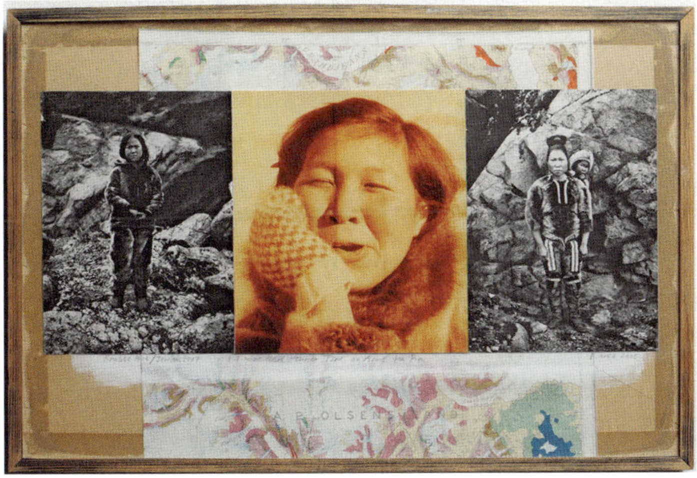

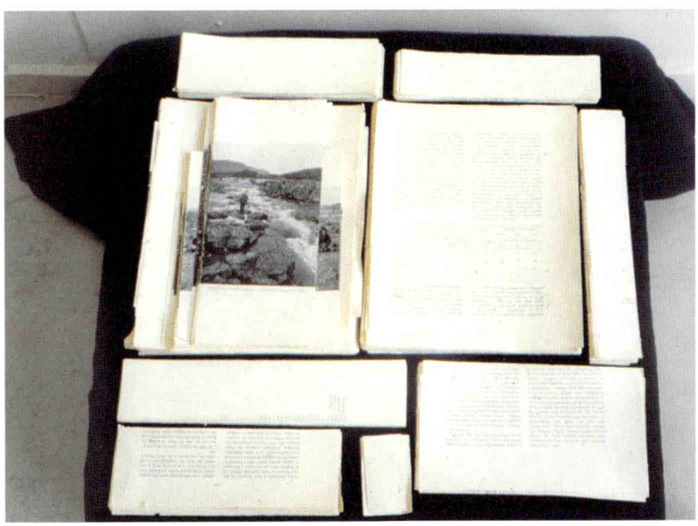

Top: *Krabbe 1906 / Jensen 1947*, 2005

Bottom: Dias 9 of 10 from *Untitled (Krabbe's Book)*, c. 1998

returns the people to a place that before had only been rendered in the maps as lines, colours and signatures. While manipulating the connection between the cartography and its implicit grounding in colonial politics, Arke also introduces a new body on top of the maps. With in-depth knowledge of the colonial power's historical archives and documents, she adds the emotional perspective of subjective history, mixing her own history with that of her mother as a young woman. Moreover, *Legend I-V* is where the artist most painfully makes us perceive the fateful interplay of the mineral and the organic – landscape and body – in her art, alongside the phenomenon of separation in the broadest possible sense. Her friend from Scoresbysund, Susanne Mortensen, dies from cancer, as Arke herself eventually did. The healing in the artwork was, and remains, a perspective on the future. That's what art can do.

Translated by Glen Garner

Right page and the next spreads:
Legend I-V, 1999

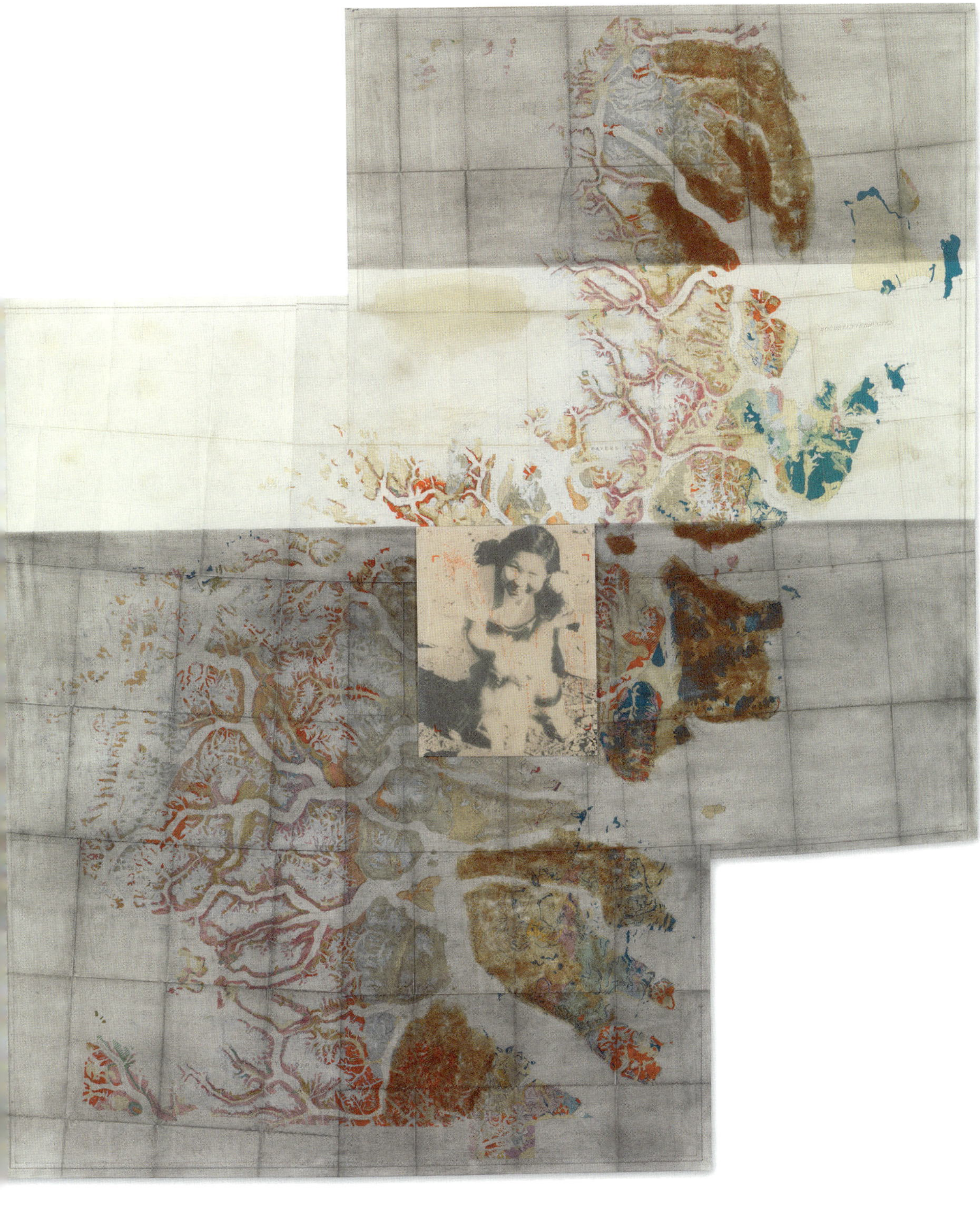

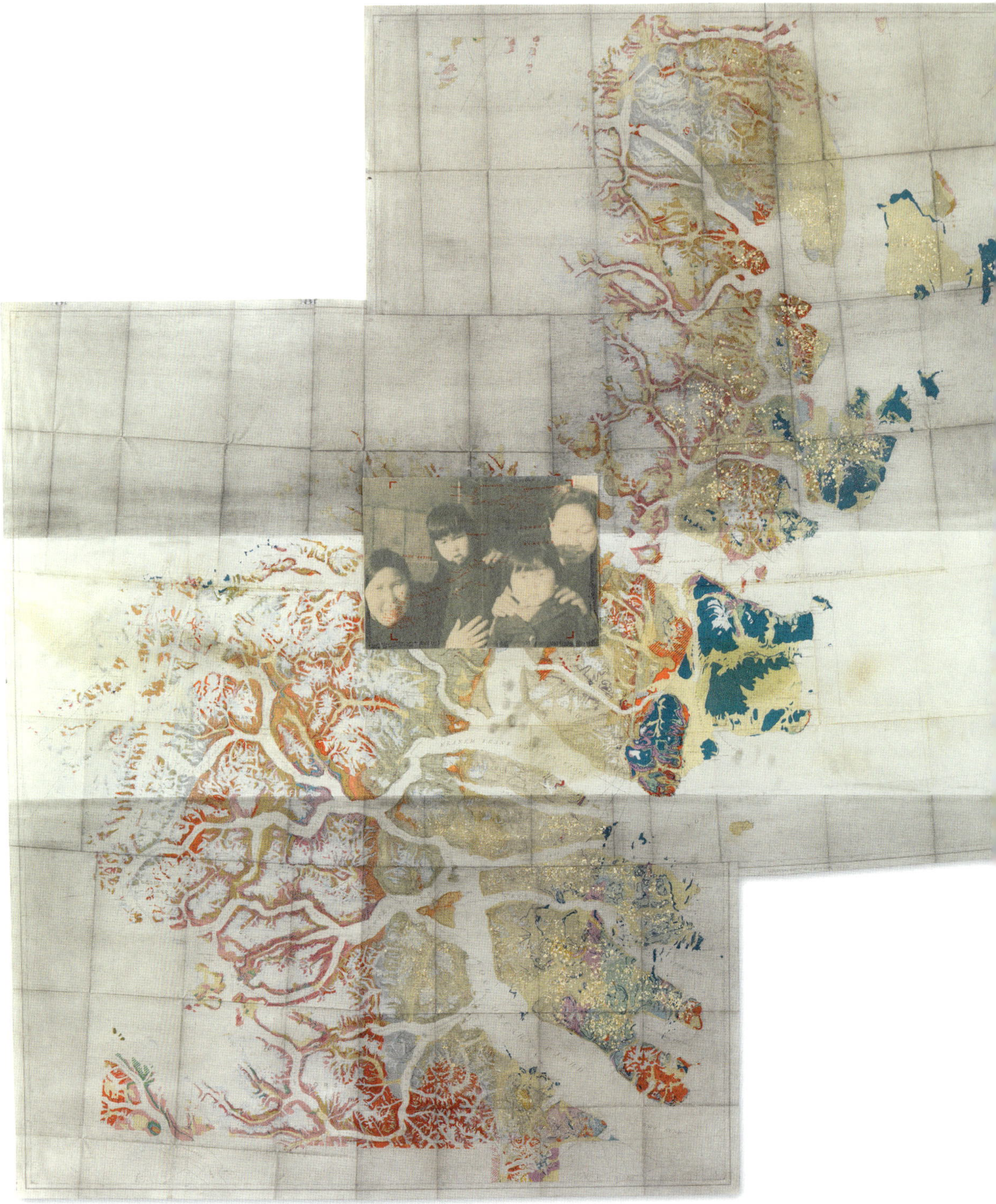

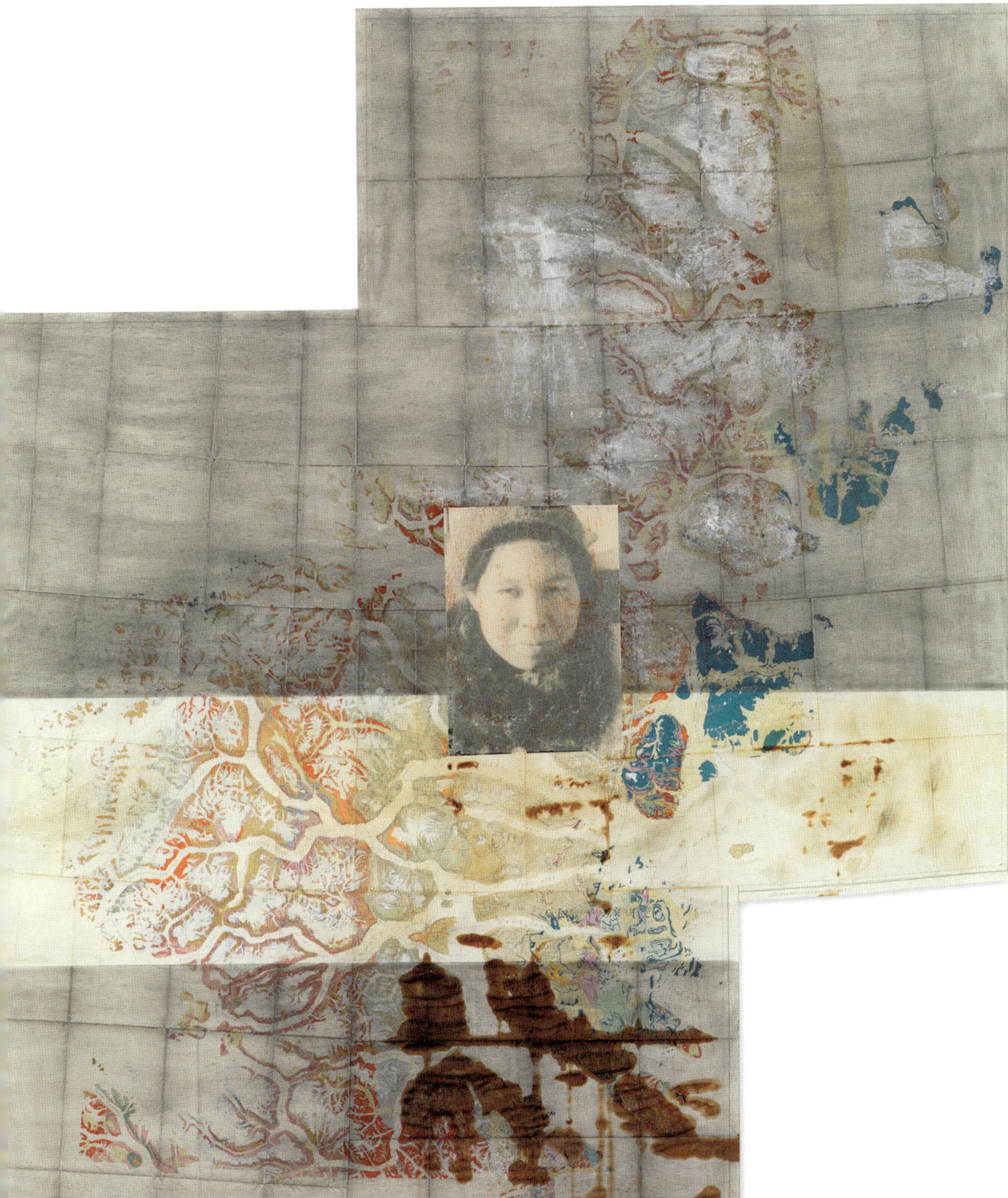

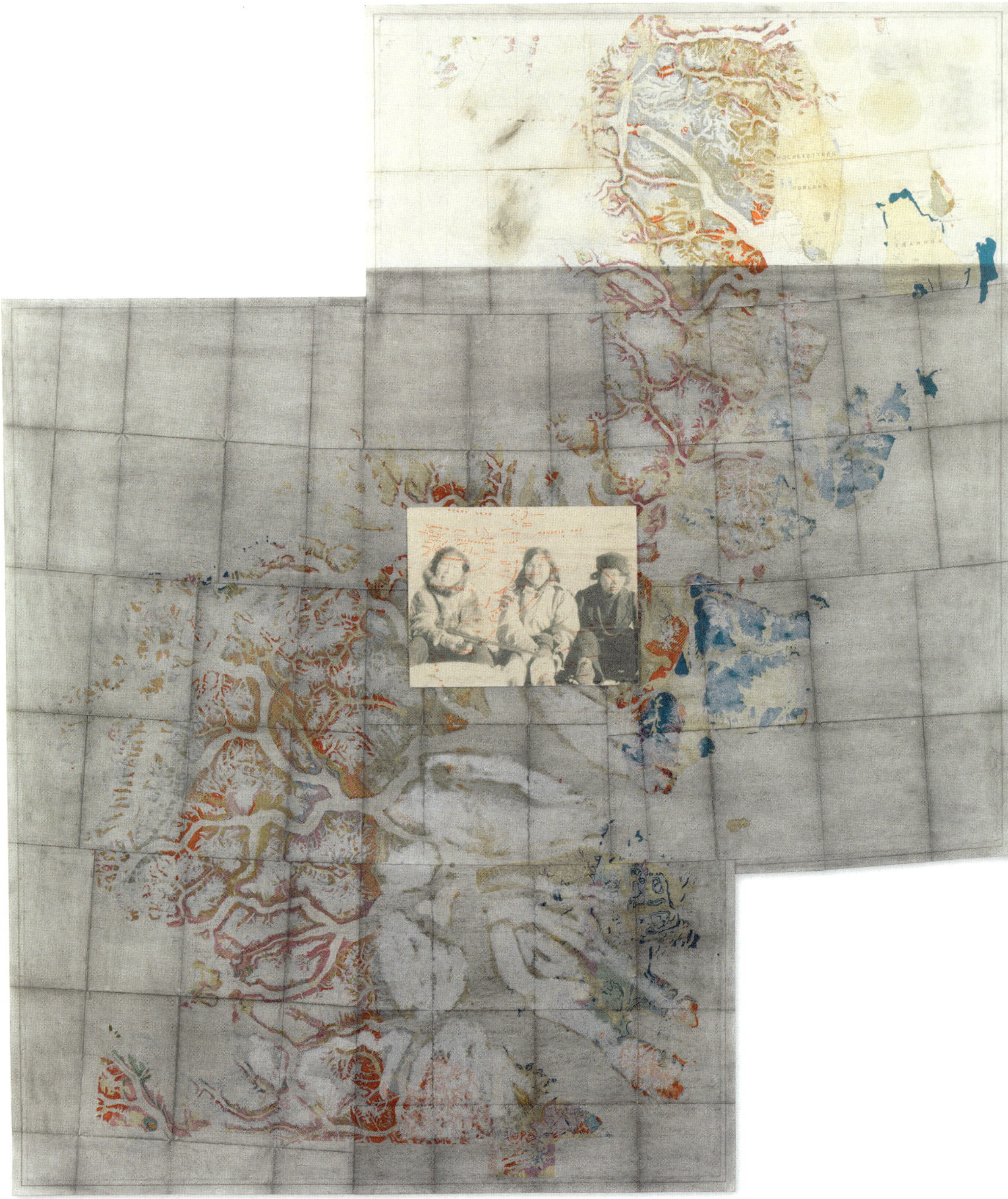

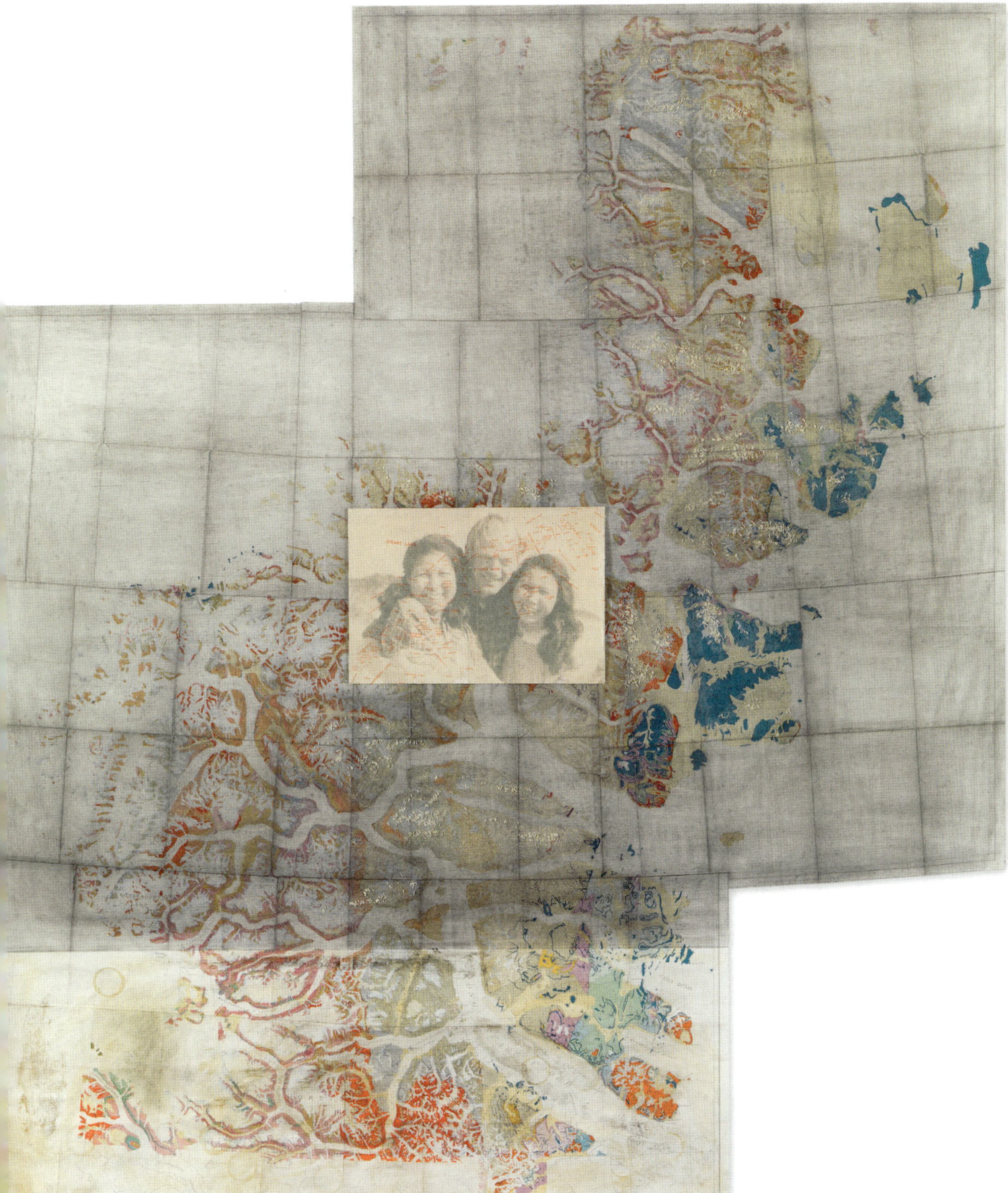

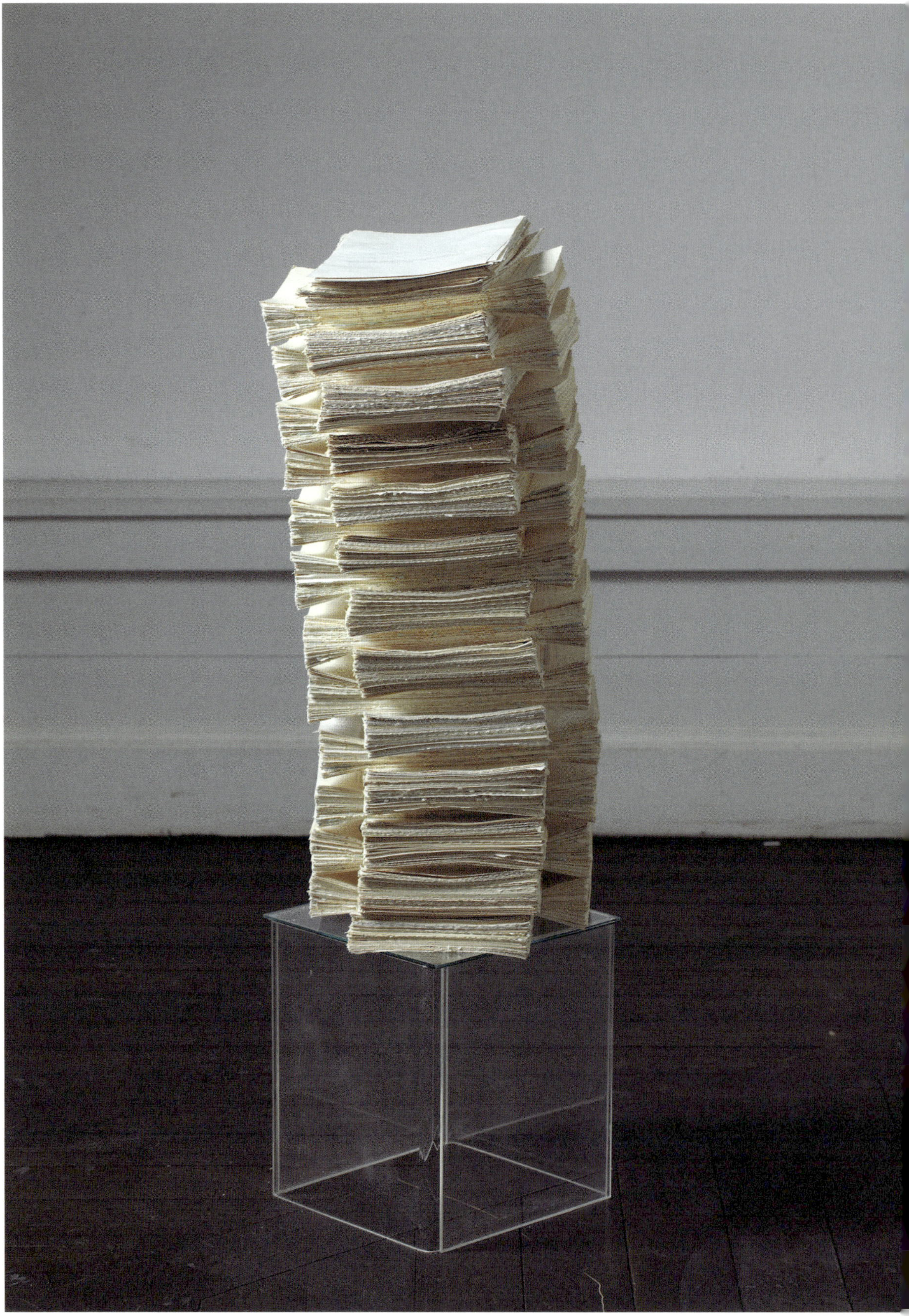

X

Tupilakosaurus:

An Animal, a Spirit, a Word

Minik Rosing

May Only Be Touched with Thumb and Little Finger, 1999

One of the most beautiful places you can find yourself is Ittoqqortoormiit, on the northern corner of Scoresby Sound Fjord in East Greenland, a small town built in the mouth of a fjord, so long it was once believed to be a sound.

In this gorgeous spot, a town of 80 people was established in 1925 as a bastion against the Norwegian ambition to annex Northeast Greenland and name it Erik the Red's Land.

A mere 40 years after Gustav Holm had been the first European to encounter the 431-strong population on the nearly 3,000 kilometre long east coast of Greenland, and just 30 years after the church and the store had come to Ammassalik, a sixth of the sparse population was relocated almost 1,000 kilometres north to what for them was an unknown place. The world's most remote town was founded.

Some probably moved north driven by the same desire that draws all explorers to the farthest corners of the world. Others tagged along, lured by the promise of a good hunt and abundant food. Yet others ended up there for reasons that were as inexplicable then as they are now.

The parents and grandparents of those who left had all been baptized in adulthood. They had grown up in a society based on hunting and fishing and eternal travel between changing winter lodgings and summer hunting grounds. They consulted shamans when beseeching nature's omnipresent spirits for aid or mercy. Throughout the summer, they gorged themselves on fat Arctic char and gave themselves over to song and the most delightful glossary of body language under the warm light of the midnight sun. They maintained justice among themselves through sharp social control. Differences were settled by mutual verbal abuse, until one party succumbed to the shame and ridicule. In case of more serious grievances, magic could be used to fabricate a monster, a *tupilak*, to kill one's foe.

Within a few decades, the East Greenlanders saw their whole worldview upended. They had become settled Christian citizens of a blooming Greenlandic nation. But no sooner had the baptismal water been wiped off their heads than trouble struck again. Now, they were caught in the crossfire of the nationalistic fervour raging in the outside world. The land in which they had always lived and travelled, the subject of the most maudlin and romantic songs imaginable, was being contested by nations all claiming it as their own. The Norwegians wanted Northeast Greenland, Peary believed North Greenland was properly his, the West

Greenlanders thought the East Greenlanders would be better off as West Greenlanders, while Denmark maintained that the whole place was Danish. Now, the small East Greenlandic population was divided in two and spread out along the coast as part of a Danish-Greenlandic bulwark against Norway's neo-Norse imperialism.

Another weapon in the fight to keep Greenland united as one nation under the Danish flag was science. In 1931, Norway declared Northeast Greenland to be conquered and two weeks later the Storting in Oslo unanimously voted to annex the area. That same summer, the geologist Lauge Koch established the geology stations Eagle's Nest, on Ella Island in divinely beautiful King Oscar Fjord (what, the Swedes now, too?), and Eskimonæs, on Clavering Island. The Lauge Koch expedition was an important step in the Danish claim to sovereignty. With funding from the Carlsberg Foundation, the Danish state and private sponsors, more than one hundred geologists, setting out from the two stations, spent three years mapping Northeast Greenland. One, the palaeontologist Eigil Nielsen, was active for all three of these years. In 1931, on a trip to Celsius Mountain, not far from the Eagle's Nest, he suddenly felt that he was being watched and found the fossilized skull of a fish staring out at him from a rock. On closer inspection, this "kalorius", or critter, as he called it, turned out not to have fins but legs for walking. Nielsen had discovered the four-legged fish, a transitional form between fish and land animals that had ambled through a tropical tidal wetland 360 million years ago, when Ittoqqortoormiit was located right on the Equator. This animal, named *Ichthyostega*, was the earliest known land animal. The opening scene of Pia Arke's film *Tupilakosaurus* shows a drawing of a fish cranium. It is actually Ichthyostega, the "kalorius" that was staring Nielsen in the neck.

From 1932–33, Nielsen spent the winter at Eskimonæs right across from imposing Cape Stosch. There he found the 200-million-year-old remains of a previously unknown ancestor of today's amphibians, an odd creature whose skeleton looked like it had been stitched together from bits and pieces of various other members of the great subphylum of vertebrates. Some parts belonged under the amphibians, while others resembled ichthyosauruses more. Nielsen, who had a terrific sense of

Next spread: Pia Arke and Anders Jørgensen: Stills from *Tupilakosaurus: An Interesting Study about the Triassic Myth of Kap Stosch*, 1999

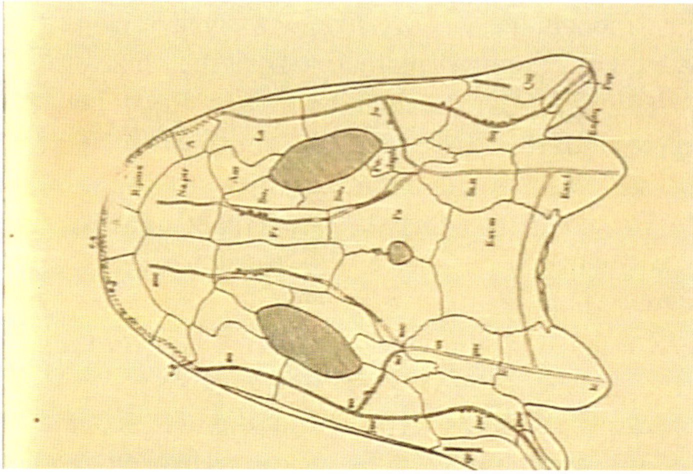

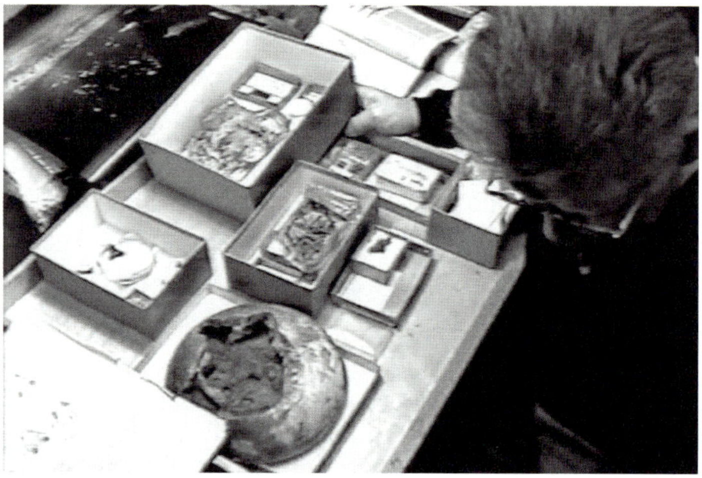

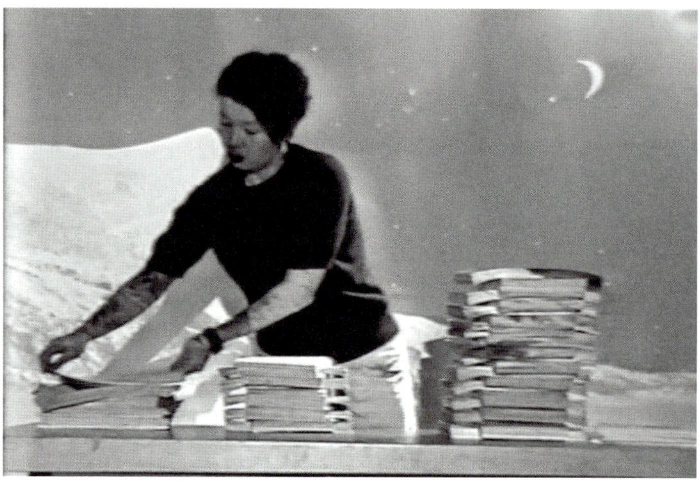

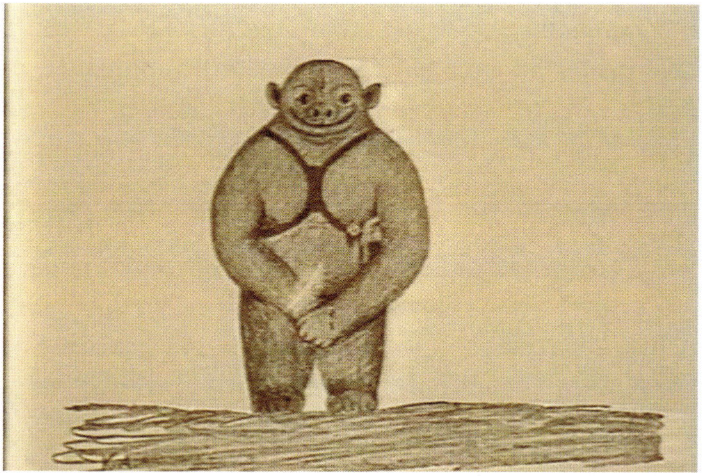

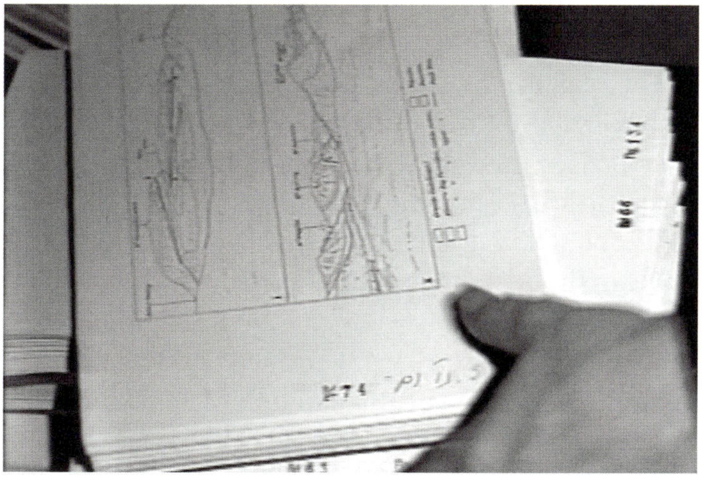

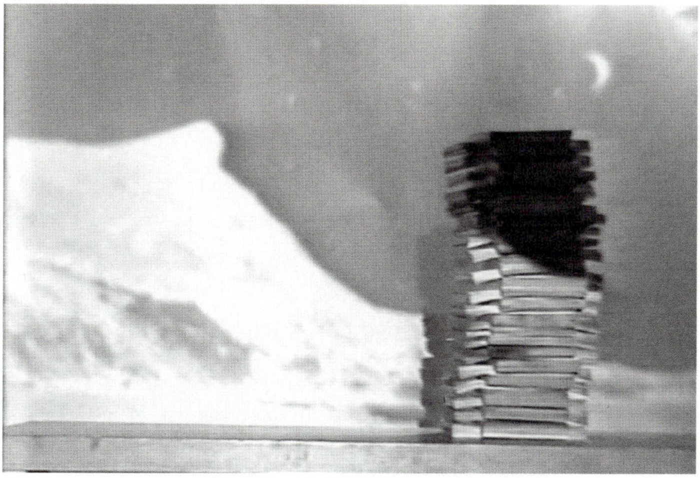

humour and a keen interest in Greenlandic culture, thought the beast should be named for the Greenlandic tupilak, which remained at large in Ittoqqortoormiit and environs. Tupilakosaurus it was.

The tupilak was a spirit being with no physical substance. To make a tupilak, you had to fabricate a physical body first, a kind of mould in which the actual tupilak, the spirit, could be conjured. The body was to be fabricated from animal or human parts, according to very detailed instructions. In an old skin, one would assemble a skeleton defining the qualities of the tupilak: the flipper of a seal, the wing of a bird, a bear bone and, most important, something belonging to the person that the tupilak was going to kill. This skeleton would then be covered in peat, seaweed or anything else that would serve as flesh. Finally, it was wrapped in the skin. In order for it to work, the whole procedure had to be performed using only one's thumb and little finger, without any of the other fingers touching the ingredients. The package then had to be buried or lowered into the sea, while a powerful incantation was recited. No effort was to be spared. For if one's foe was wielding more powerful magic, he could send the tupilak back to kill the original sender. Once the tupilak was created, it was no longer bound by its physical form. On the other hand, it could avail itself only of the qualities its creator had endowed it with in its skin bundle.

Because a tupilak was a spirit being with no physical manifestation, it was hard for missionaries, whalers and traders to fully understand what a tupilak was and why people were so afraid of it. The East Greenlanders had no tradition of drawing, but they were formidably skilled at carving ivory, wood or bone, and so the tradition of tupilak figures was born. The tupilak figure is simply an illustration of the form of the spirit in question, a catalogue of its inherent powers. The tupilak itself, no one can see.

The film *Tupilakosaurus* is part of Pia Arke's great reckoning with outside observers and the boundless need of internal moralizers to define what a real Greenlander is. She found the post-colonial fight over Greenlandishness suffocating and oppressive to her own, entirely reasonable, wish to define herself.

As a child, Arke would lie on the bed platform, the heart of any Greenlandic home, and sense the gentle light of the East Greenlandic night creeping in the windows. Half asleep she would hear her mother and her mother's friends talking, singing and howling with laughter.

East Greenlandic is utterly, indescribably beautiful. Like a rock tumbling in the waves, a millennium of daily use has worn the sharp edges off the language. What remains is the solid core of meaning, in its softest, most ergonomic form. When a group of East Greenlanders talk with each other, it is often in such a singularly quiet and calm tone of voice that you don't always notice when speech turns into song, and vice versa.

Arke never learned her mother tongue, or West Greenlandic, despite a deep longing to know the language of her Greenlandic identity. I think, if you have spent your early childhood with another language spoken around you, you will always be able to understand the meaning of what is being said, even if you don't understand the actual words. Conversely, you can learn to speak another language as an adult and understand all the words without ever really being able to understand the meaning. Arke understood East Greenlandic, even if she didn't speak it.

Arke was immersed in the science that had been conducted around her childhood fjord, and she was entranced by the stunningly beautiful geological maps of the area that science had produced – maps full of strange words and names that are ripe with meaning to the initiated, who know the history of the European exploration of East Greenland, but are utter nonsense to those who live there. With the Greenlandic knack for laughing at things that could just as easily make you cry, Arke exposes the profound comedy she saw in the scientific approach to understanding and describing the world. At the same time, she was genuinely fascinated by the stories that science extracts from the hard rock of the mountains and the delightful forms that cartographers translate the country into in their maps.

Cape Stosch, which appears in *Tupilakosaurus*, is a good example. This poor, old cape was named after a German admiral by random German passersby pluckily attempting to reach the North Pole.

A map is a way of giving concrete expression to the shape and physical composition of a landscape, but it does not necessarily include any actual knowledge of the land. A map is also the authorized way of claiming ownership of a territory. He who makes the map, naming places in print, is the rightful owner of the land, according to international law.

Nomadic people know their land inside and out, and name places after phenomena that are important to them personally, without expecting others to share their taste or abide by their choices. They know the good places to be, without necessarily being able to say exactly what makes a place good. They know the land and can navigate it without a map, with a clear GPS-like sense of where they are. The land owns itself and no one is arrogant enough to presume that they can own a land. Thus, Arke puts her tragicomic spin on maps. On the one hand, a map is a document of the intrinsic human curiosity and desire to explore the world. On the other hand, it is a legal document that makes some people feel entitled to submit another country to their will for the simple reason that they know what it looks like, even if they don't know the slightest thing about the country or the people in it.

Translated by Glen Garner

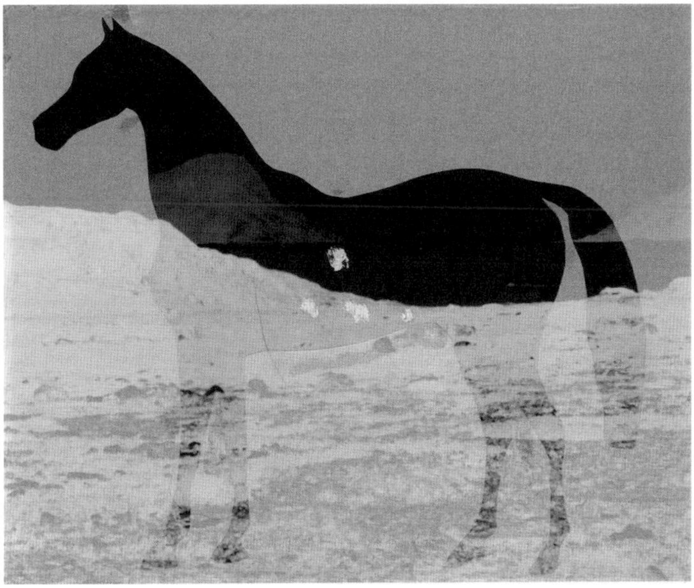

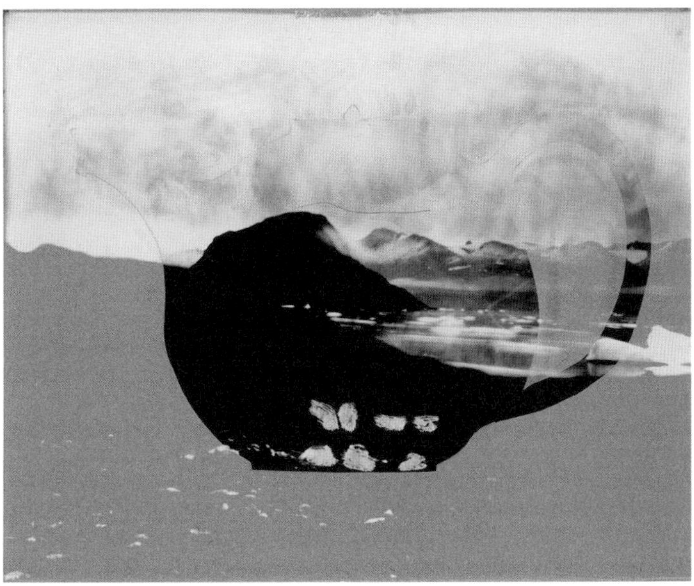

Top: *Untitled (Pinhole Camera Photograph with "Horse")*,
c. 1990-1995

Bottom: *Untitled (Pinhole Camera Photograph with "Teapot")*,
c. 1990-1995

Notes

Page 21. The Arctic Portal. Anders Kold

1. Several of the writers of this volume describe Arke's practice as artistic research and as an attempt to establish an artistic practice that speaks from a third position, between art and science. Kuratorisk Aktion's framing of the 2010 exhibition, its design and communication, was likewise inspired by central aspects of artistic research. Symptomatically, the exhibition made a detour to the National Museum's collection of Greenlandic objects. Post-colonial theorizing has seen a shift since the 2010 Arke exhibition and publication, and the term "decolonial" has become widely prevalent in the research community, replacing "post-colonial".

2. This phenomenon is central to several branches of humanities research. Introducing the concept in his *Performativ biografisme. En hovedstrømning i den senmoderne skandinaviske litteratur* (2014), literature scholar Jon Helt Haarder applies the phenomenon in a broader cultural perspective. In the intersection of fiction and reality, hybrid representations of the biographical material are playfully performed.

3. "Det mørke kammer", interview with Synne Rifbjerg, *Weekendavisen*, 29 April – 6 May 1999, p. 11.

4. In the archives of the Arke Estate are negatives from a third, never realized series, which was taken in the apartment in 1989 and mixes elements of the other two.

5. In *Tupilakosaurus*, p. 93, Kuratorisk Aktion finds that Arke's abandonment of painting was less categorical. I find this viewpoint to be informed more by a general resistance to traditional-historical analysis than by a convincing exemplification. Excepting the commissions Arke took on after 1990, the remaining volume of her paintings is not significant to her work.

6. Arke, quoted in Stefan Jonsson, *Förbundna i tystnad. Pia Arke utforskar banden mellem Grönland och Danmark*, *Dagens Nyheter*, 18 March 1995. The term also appears in the artist's brother, Erik Gant's, cover copy for Arke's *Etnoæstetik*, Copenhagen, also 1995.

7. Iben Mondrup, "The Postcolonial Body in Pia Arke's Work", in *Tupilakosaurus*, p. 293-298. As Mondrup writes, archives were both the source and the target of Arke's artistic research, and were seriously tested by her art. This did not happen until 1993, however, when Arke was admitted to the Academy of Fine Arts' Department of Aesthetics and Communication, under the direction of Associate Professor Carsten Juhl, from which she graduated in 1995 with her thesis project *Etnoæstetik*.

8. In the archives of the Arke Estate is a series of slides Arke must have taken of the six printed photographs. In them, an additional subject appears, whose pose matches a 1992 *Self-Portrait* at the Royal Library. Hence, the artist must also have made a black-and-white print of this subject, which presumably was given away or has been lost.

9. *Rygskriver*, a 1985 photograph by the artist Kirsten Justesen, shows her sitting naked on the ice in Greenland, writing on her own back. The similarity is obvious and Arke was undoubtedly familiar with this work. However, Justesen's photos are bound up with and thematize a sculptural practice, while Arke's works point in a different direction. At stake is the issue of identity, and here Arke's connection to the ice of Greenland is of another nature.

10. This work was first shown at Hallwalls, an alternative arts centre in Buffalo, NY, and was not shown again until 2007 in connection with the publication of a book.

11. Arke may have seen Sherman's *Untitled Film Stills* at the Louisiana in 1984, and in 1988 at the *Matris* exhibition at Malmö Konstmuseum, while she was attending the Academy of Fine Arts. Both exhibitions included the category "Rear Screen Projections", with Sherman posing in front of a projected image.

12. These photos bring to mind the experimental photography practice of the Danish artist Richard Winther, who began reinterpreting classical art in the mid-1960s. Arke's photos can be dated to late 1988 or January 1989.

13. The first apartment is on Griffenfeldsgade in Nørrebro, the other on Nyelandsvej in Frederiksberg.

14. This is merely to note that the presence of a map, a flat section of a landscape, intriguingly undergirds the artist's 1999 key work *Legende I-V*, in which Danish photographs of Greenlanders, taken in 1947, are symbolically overlaid on official maps of Scoresby Sound, the area of northeast Greenland where Arke was born and lived until she was four years old.

15. Artist's statement for an exhibition (with Fie Johansen) of the pinhole camera box and six pinhole photographs of Narsaq, at Albertslund Town Hall, April-May 1994.

16. Erik Gant, "Work and Reality", in *The Return of the Past. The End of Utopias?*, p.58, Ars Baltica, 1st Baltic Triennial of Photography, 1996.

Researching this essay, I spoke with artists who knew Arke. I would like to thank Per Bak Jensen, Sophia Kalkau, Lotte Tauber Lassen, Erik Steffensen, Tina Schwarz and Lars Schwander. Thanks as well to Mette Sandbye, Niels Boe Havgaard, Bruun-Rasmussen Auctioneers of Fine Art and thesis student Helle Fagralid. A special word of gratitude to Søren Arke and his father, Michael Petersen.

Page 39. For Those Who Live on the Shoreline. Laura Smith

1. Virginia Woolf, *To the Lighthouse*, p.87.

2. Kuratorisk Aktion, *TUPILAKOSAURUS: Pia Arke's Issue with Art, Ethnicity, and Colonialism, 1981-2006*, p.74.

3. Catherine Clément and Hélène Cixous, *The Newly Born Woman*, 1975.

4. Clément and Cixous, *The Newly Born Woman*, 1975.

5. Audre Lorde, excerpt from 'A Litany for Survival', 1978, from *The Collected Poems of Audre Lorde*, 1997.

6. Kuratorisk Aktion, *TUPILAKOSAURUS: Pia Arke's Issue with Art, Ethnicity, and Colonialism, 1981-2006*, p.8.

Page 83. Body and Map. Anders Kold

1. In *Tupilakosaurus* (p.256), Finn Thrane points out that *Nature Morte* alias *Perlustrations 1-10* in a wider sense links Susanne Mortensen's body to a traumatic state between two cultures. Likewise, in the same publication (p.316), Stefan Jonsson connects mutilation to how colonialism robbed them both of their mother tongue and their past.

2. The invention of the diorama is attributed to the French painter and pioneer of photography Louis Daguerre.

List of Works

Untitled (Pencil Self-Portrait), c. mid 1980s
Pencil on paper
23 × 15 cm
Private collection

Flensing of Seal, 1987
Acrylic on canvas
100 × 120.5 cm
Private collection

Camel in Snowscape, 1987
Oil on cardboard
15.5 × 25.4 cm
Collection of Stefan Jonsson

Untitled (Small Camera Obscura), 1988–1990
Colour print from slide
21 × 29.7 cm
Pia Arke Estate

Untitled (Small Camera Obscura Photographs), c. 1988–1990
Series of 3 black-and-white photographs
Each: 11 × 13.5 cm
Pia Arke Estate

Untitled (Self-Portrait, Undressing in Interior), c. 1989
Series of 6 black-and-white photographs, print (2021) after negatives in Pia Arke Estate
Each: 17.8 × 9 cm
Pia Arke Estate

Camera Obscura, 1990
Printed invitation to the inauguration of the Camera Obscura
21 × 14.8 cm (A5)
Nuuk Art Museum

Untitled (Camera Obscura), 1990
Black-and-white photograph
7.3 × 7.3 cm
Nuuk Art Museum

Untitled (Drawing Plan for Large Camera Obscura), 1990
Pencil, pen, marker and paint on paper
28.3 × 33.9 cm
Nuuk Art Museum

Nuugaarsuk alias *Pinhole Camera Photograph* alias *The Point*, 1990
Silver gelatin print on baryte paper
49 × 59 cm
Louisiana Museum of Modern Art
Acquired with funding from The Augustinus Foundation

Nuugaarsuk alias *Pinhole Camera Photograph* alias *The Point*, 1990
Series of 4 gelatin silver prints on baryte paper
Each: 49.5 × 59.5 cm
Kunstmuseum Brandts

Side by Side, early 1990s
Diptych consisting of gelatin silver print on baryte paper photographed with pinhole camera and colour toned photograph mounted on cardboard with pencil annotations
Each: 56.5 × 68 cm
Private collection

Untitled (Pinhole Camera Photograph with "Horse"), c. 1990–1995
Parchment paper, paint and hair on pinhole camera negative
49 × 58.5 cm
Louisiana Museum of Modern Art
Acquired with funding from The Augustinus Foundation

Untitled (Pinhole Camera Photograph with "Teapot"), c. 1990–1995
Parchment paper, paint and hair on silver gelatin baryte paper
48.8 × 59 cm
Louisiana Museum of Modern Art
Acquired with funding from The Augustinus Foundation

Untitled (Pinhole Camera Photograph with Plant Tracing), c. 1990
Black-and-white photograph with pencil and white paint
24 × 30.5 cm
Royal Danish Library

Self-Portrait, 1992
Black-and-white photograph
12.5 × 10 cm
Private collection

Self-Portrait, 1992
Double exposure black-and-white photograph, 17.2 × 17.2 cm
Private collection

Self-Portrait, 1992
Double exposure black-and-white photograph, 30 × 25 cm
Private collection

Self-Portrait with Cousin, 1992
2 silver gelatin prints on paper
Each: 22.5 × 6.7 cm
Louisiana Museum of Modern Art
Acquired with funding from The Augustinus Foundation

Old School Map, c. 1992
Pencil on parchment paper on map
64.5 × 47.2 cm
Nuuk Art Museum

Untitled (Pinhole Camera Negative), c. 1992
Pinhole camera negative
50 × 60 cm
Pia Arke Estate

Imaginary Homelands alias *Ultima Thule* alias *Dundas "The Old Thule"*, 1992/2003
Series of 4 silver gelatin prints in white frames with pencil annotations
Individual dimensions (framed):
46 × 44 × 1 cm / 55.4 × 43.4 × 1 cm / 46 × 56.5 × 1 cm / 44 × 47 × 1 cm
Louisiana Museum of Modern Art
Acquired with funding from Anker Fonden

The Three Graces, 1993
Series of 4 gelatin silver prints on baryte paper
Individual dimensions:
110.6 × 90.4 cm / 110.7 × 91.9 cm / 111 × 91. 3 / 110.1 × 90.3 cm
Kunstmuseum Brandts

Untitled (Put your Kamik on your Head so Everyone Can See where You Come from), c. 1993
Black-and-white contact sheet
20 × 15 cm
Malmö Art Museum, Sweden

Untitled (Toying with National Costume), c. 1993
Black-and-white contact sheet
20 × 15 cm
Malmö Art Museum, Sweden

Nature Morte alias *Perlustrations 1-10*, 1994
Series of 10 gelatin silver prints on baryte paper
43 × 52 cm
Kunstmuseum Brandts

Untitled (The Three Graces Collage), 1994
11 × 23 × 0.3 cm
Black-and-white photo collage mounted on cardboard
Louisiana Museum of Modern Art
Acquired with funding from The Augustinus Foundation

Scoresbysund 1947, c. 1995
Yellow toned photograph
68.8 × 102.6 cm
Pia Arke Estate

Untitled (Sven Lund Jensen's Photo Album), c. 1995
45 slides
Pia Arke Estate

Wonderland, 1996
Inkjet print
79.9 × 150 cm
Kunstmuseum Brandts

Telegraphy, 1996
18 photographs
Each: 28.8 × 40.5 cm
Pia Arke Estate

Arctic Hysteria, 1996
Video 4:3 (S-VHS video to DVD)
Duration: 5:55 min
Louisiana Museum of Modern Art
Acquired with funding from Anker Fonden

Untitled (Arctic Hysteria sketch), c. 1996-1997
Digitalized photo of lost sketch for *Arctic Hysteria IV*
Dimensions variable
Nuuk Art Museum

Untitled (Register on Image Proof Sheets), 1997-2003
Typed and handwritten text on different paper types
Pia Arke Estate

Untitled (Scoresbysund Panorama), c. 1997-2001
Series of 4 black-and-white photographs with black marker annotations
Individual dimensions (framed): 16 × 12 cm / 15.9 × 16.5 cm / 16.5 × 15.9 cm / 16.5 × 16.5 cm
Nuuk Art Museum

Dummy, 1997-2003
49 framed collages consisting of post-its with handwritten notes attached to dummy sheets from Pia Arke's original dummy for her book work *Stories from Scoresbysund: Photographs, Colonisation and Mapping*, Borgen, 2003
Each (framed): 24.5 × 42 cm
Nuuk Art Museum

Uden titel (Dummy), 1997-2003
6 framed collages consisting of post-its with handwritten notes attached to dummy sheets from Pia Arke's original dummy for her book work *Stories from Scoresbysund: Photographs, Colonisation and Mapping*, Borgen, 2003
Each (framed): 24.5 × 42 cm
Private collection

Key Map, 1997-2003
Composite archival document with notes by the artist, print, pencil and ballpoint pen on paper
29.5 × 84 cm
Louisiana Museum of Modern Art
Acquired with funding from The Augustinus Foundation

The Shadow of a Hopeful Photographer in an Ice Desert, 1998
Image proof sheet from the monograph series *Meddelelser om Grønland* (Monographs on Greenland) placed inside portfolio from Lauge Koch & John Haller's book *Geological Map of East Greenland 72°-76° N. Lat.*, C.A. Reitzel Publisher, 1971
28 × 18 × 2 cm
Collection of Lars Kiel Bertelsen

Krabbe's Book, c. 1998
C-print
Series of 6 photographs (colour)
Each: 11.5 × 9 cm
Louisiana Museum of Modern Art
Acquired with funding from Anker Fonden

Untitled (Krabbe's Book), c. 1998
Series of 10 colour slides
Louisiana Museum of Modern Art
Acquired with funding from Anker Fonden

Pia Arke and Anders Jørgensen
Tupilakosaurus: An Interesting Study about the Triassic Myth of Kap Stosch, 1999
Video 4:3 (S-VHS video to DVD)
Duration: 9:18 min
Pia Arke Estate

May Only Be Touched with Thumb and Little Finger, 1999
Ready-made, book blocks from *Meddelelser om Grønland* (Monographs on Greenland)
120 × 45 × 45 cm
Pia Arke Estate

Legend I-V, 1999
Collage: Paper, pencil, pen, gelatin silver print, wood, flour, coffee, sugar, oat flakes and rice
5 parts, each: 197 × 165 cm
Louisiana Museum of Modern Art
Acquired with funding from Anker Fonden

Krabbe 1906 / Jensen 1947, 2005
Collage consisting of photographs and a map
Framed: 31 × 45 cm
Private collection

Books and catalogues:

ATTACK!, 1999
Pia Arke's contribution to the exhibition catalogue for the exhibition *ATTACK! Photography on the Edge*, Antwerpen & Baarn: Houtekiet & De Prom, 1999
Pia Arke Estate

Scoresbysundhistorier: Fotografier, kolonisering og kortlægning, Borgen, 2003
Stories from Scoresbysund: Photographs, Colonisation and Mapping

Reproductions:

Untitled (Self-Portrait, Undressing in Interior), c. 1989
Reproduction from slide
Pia Arke Estate

Untitled (Double Exposure Self-Portrait in Interior), 1990
4 reproductions from slide
Pia Arke Estate

Untitled (Pibloctoq-Arctic Hysteria Archive), 1995

Reproduction from slide
21 × 29.7 cm
Pia Arke Estate

Arctic Hysteria IV, 1997
(original lost, reproduction 2010)
Reproduction: Yellow toned photomontage
79.3 × 202.5 cm
Louisiana Museum of Modern Art

Works in Public Collections

Denmark

Aarhus University

Department of Bioscience, Roskilde

Untitled (Composition with Narwhal and Seal), 2001
Oil and pen on canvas
Framed: 85.5 × 76.5 cm

Untitled (Composition with Yellow Polar Bear), 2001
Oil on canvas
Framed: 80.5 × 99.2 cm

Kunstmuseum Brandts

Nuugaarsuk alias *Pinhole Camera Photograph* alias *The Point*, 1990
4 silver gelatin prints on baryte paper
Each: 49.5 × 59.5 cm
Inv.no. 94-018-01-04

The Three Graces, 1993
4 silver gelatin prints on baryte paper
Individual dimensions:
110.6 × 90.4 cm / 110.7 × 91.9 cm / 111 × 91.3 cm / 110.1 × 90.3 cm
Inv.no. 09-116-01-04

Nature Morte alias *Perlustrations 1-10*, 1994
10 silver gelatin prints on baryte paper
Each: 43 × 52 cm
Inv.no. 95-05-9-01-10

Wonderland, 1996
Inkjet print
79.9 × 150 cm
Inv.no. 09-118

Louisiana Museum of Modern Art

Nuugaarsuk alias *Pinhole Camera Photograph* alias *The Point*, 1990
Silver gelatin print on baryte paper
49.5 × 59.5 cm
Acquired with funding from The Augustinus Foundation

Untitled (Pinhole Camera Photograph with "Horse"), early 1990s
Parchment paper, paint and hair on pinhole camera negative
49 × 58.5 cm
Acquired with funding from The Augustinus Foundation

Untitled (Pinhole Camera Photograph with "Teapot"), early 1990s
Parchment paper, paint, and hair on silver gelatin baryte paper
48.8 × 59 cm
Acquired with funding from The Augustinus Foundation

Self-Portrait with Cousin, 1992
2 silver gelatin prints on paper
Each: 22.5 × 6.7 cm
Acquired with funding from The Augustinus Foundation

Imaginary Homelands alias *Ultima Thule* alias *Dundas "The Old Thule"*, 1992/2003
4 silver gelatin prints in white frames with pencil annotations
Individual dimensions (framed):
46 × 44 × 1 cm / 55.4 × 43.4 × 1 cm / 46 × 56.5 × 1 cm / 44 × 47 × 1 cm
Acquired with funding from Anker Fonden

Untitled (The Three Graces Collage), 1994
Photo collage mounted on cardboard
11 × 23 × 0.3 cm
Acquired with funding from The Augustinus Foundation

Arctic Hysteria, 1996
Video 4:3 (S-VHS video to DVD)
Duration 5:55 min
Acquired with funding from Anker Fonden

Key Map, 1997-2003
Print, pencil and ballpoint pen on paper
29.5 × 84 cm
Acquired with funding from The Augustinus Foundation

Krabbe's Book, c. 1998
C-print
6 photographs, colour
Each: 11.5 × 9 cm
Acquired with funding from Anker Fonden

Untitled (Krabbe's Book), c. 1998
Series of 10 colour slides
Acquired with funding from Anker Fonden

Legende I-V, 1999
Legend I-V
Collage: Paper, pencil, pen, gelatin silver print, wood, flour, coffee, sugar, oat flakes and rice
5 parts, each: 197 × 165 cm
Acquired with funding from Anker Fonden

The Danish National Art Library

The Daily Actions, 1989
4 colour photographs (in a series of 7)
Each: 10 × 15 cm
Inv.no. 58191

The National Collection of Photography, The Royal Danish Library

Untitled (Leporello Self-Portrait), c. 1987
Black-and-white leporello photograph with 6 images
12.5 × 66.2 cm
Inv.no. 2013-99/1

The Point / Narsaq, 1990
Silver gelatin print on baryte paper
49.9 × 59.2 cm
Inv.no. 1992-984/1-2

Untitled (Pinhole Camera Photograph with Plant Tracing), c. 1990
Black-and-white photograph with pencil and white paint
24 × 30.5 cm
Inv.no. 2013-99/6

Dundas "The Old Thule", 1992
4 silver gelatin prints on baryte paper
Individual dimensions:
44.5 × 53.8 cm / 45 × 55 cm / 44.3 × 53.5 cm / 44.5 × 54.0 cm
Inv.no. 1992-1012/1-4

Self-Portrait, 1992
Double exposure black-and-white self-portrait superimposed over pinhole camera photograph
30.2 × 25.0 cm
Inv.no. 2013-99/2

Self-Portrait, 1992
Double exposure black-and-white self-portrait superimposed over pinhole camera photograph
Framed: 33.4 × 27 cm
Inv.no. 2019-31/1

Self-Portrait, 1992
Double exposure black-and-white self-portrait superimposed over pinhole camera photograph
Framed: 58 × 49.3 cm
Inv.no. 2019-31/2

The Point / Narsaq, 1992
Silver gelatin print on baryte paper
50.5 × 60.4
Inv.no. 1992-984/2

Untitled (Put Your Kamik on Your Head so Everyone Can See Where You Come From), 1993
Black-and-white contact sheet
12.7 × 12.6 cm
Inv.no. 2013-99/7

Untitled (Self-Portrait, Inuit Drum Dance), c. 1993
4 contact prints (colour)
16.6 × 38.0 cm (total)
Inv.no. 2013-99/8

Landfall I-III, 1993/2003
3 black-and-white photographs with pencil annotations
Individual dimensions:
39.2 × 48.2 cm / 43.5 × 52.2 cm / 40.3 × 25.0 cm
Inv.no. 2013-99/3-5

Nature Morte alias *Perlustrations 1-10*, 1994
10 silver gelatin prints on baryte paper
Dimension variable
Inv.no. 1994-852/1-10

Between Two Chairs, 1996
Pinhole camera photograph (colour)
49.7 × 60.3 cm
Inv.no. 2013-99/9

Telegraphy, 1996
18 photographs
Each: 40.5 × 28.8 / 28.8 × 40.5 cm
Inv.no. 1997-252/1-18

Gone with the Wind, 1997
Colour photograph
46.4 × 64.1 cm
Inv.no. 2018-48/1

Krabbe/Jensen, 1997
C-print photo montage
101.5 × 171.6 cm
Inv.no. 1998-173

Works in Public Collections

Untitled (Telegraphy), c. 1997
Coffee and sugar glued on to blue-toned photograph
27 × 32 cm
Inv.no. 2013-99/20

Walrus Bay 1944 and 2001, 2001-2003
Series of 10 photographs in black-and-white and colour with annotations in pencil and black marker
Dimensions variable
Inv.no. 2013-99/10-19

The North Atlantic House, Copenhagen

Untitled (Composition with Utensils), 1993
Acrylics on canvas
Framed: 204 × 289 cm
Public Collection, Long-term loan to the North Atlantic House, Copenhagen

SMK, National Gallery of Denmark

Old School Map, 1991-1992
Black-and-white photograph with blue pencil annotations on parchment paper
30 × 27 cm
Object number: KKS2019-84

Self-Portrait with Cousin, 1991-1992
Double exposure black-and-white photograph
12.5 × 10 cm
Object number: KKS2019-83

Untitled (Thule Air Base), *1991-1992*, 2002-2003
Black-and-white photograph with folding traces and frame with pencil annotations
46.5 × 56.5 cm
Object number: KKS2019-85

Untitled (An Arctic Bronze), 1994-1998
Yellow toned black-and-white photograph
128 × 79.5 cm
Object number: KKS2019-88

Untitled (Mother of the Seals (An Eskimo Legend), 1994-1998
Yellow toned black-and-white photograph
67 × 92 cm
Object number: KKS2019-87

The Kronborg Series alias *The Kronborg Suite*, 1995-1996
3 silver gelatin pinhole camera photographs
Each 49.8 × 59.5 cm
Object number: KKS2019-86/1-3

The Arctic Institute, Copenhagen

Untitled (Composition with Polar Bears and Seals), 1993
Acrylics on canvas
120 × 240.5 cm

University of Copenhagen

Greenlandic and Arctic Studies, Department of Cross-Cultural and Regional Studies

Untitled, 1993
Acrylics on canvas
47 × 22.5 cm
Untitled, 1993
Oil on canvas
33 × 22.5

Greenland

Greenland National Gallery of Art

The Necromancer's Journey to the Moon, c. 1988
Colour transparency in lightbox
87 × 129 × 15 cm

Greenland National Museum & Archives

The Hunter and His Wife alias *Hunter and Wife, Past and Present*, 1988
Lithograph, 21/50
61.5 × 52.5 cm

Greenlandic Representative Office in Copenhagen, Denmark

The Hunter and His Wife alias *Hunter and Wife, Past and Present*, 1988
Lithograph, 2/50
Framed: 75.5 × 6.7 cm

Composition with Animals, 1993
Acrylics on canvas
Framed: 46 × 58 cm

Drive in Old Landscape, 1993
Mixed media,
29.5 × 28 cm

View over Old Landscape, 1993
Mixed media
30 × 28 cm

Narsaq Museum

Nuugaarsuk alias *Pinhole Camera Photograph* alias *The Point*, 1990
Silver gelatin print on baryte paper
49.5 × 59.5 cm

Nuuk Art Museum

Camera Obscura, 1990
Printed invitation to the inauguration of the Camera Obscura
21 × 14,8 cm (A5)

Untitled (Camera Obscura), 1990
Black-and-white photograph
7,3 × 7,3 cm

Untitled (Drawing Plan for Large Camera Obscura), 1990
Pencil, pen, marker and paint on paper
28.3 × 33.9 cm

Old School Map, c. 1992
Pencil on parchment paper on map
64.5 × 47.2 cm

Untitled (Thule Collectors),
1992-1993
Black-and-white photographs of
Thule collectors holding their
Pia Arke prints
4 parts with individual
dimensions: 31 × 26.5 cm /
31 × 25,5 cm / 26.3 × 32.5 cm /
31 × 26,5 cm

*Untitled (The Three Graces
Contact Sheets)*, 1993
Two Contact Sheets
Framed: 20 × 30 cm

Arctic Hysteria, 1996
Video 4:3 (S-VHS video to DVD)
Duration: 5:55 min
The Art Historian, 1996
Pinhole camera photograph
(colour)
50 × 60.5 cm

*Untitled (Arctic Hysteria
sketch)*, c. 1996-1997
Dias of lost original; collage
sketch for the photo montage
Arctic Hysteria
Dimensions variable
Gone with the Wind, 1997
Colour photograph
12.5 × 17 cm

*Untitled (Scoresbysund
Panorama)*, c. 1997-2001
Series of 4 black-and-white
photographs with black marker
annotations
Individual dimensions (framed):
16 × 12 cm / 15.9 × 16.5 cm /
16.5 × 15.9 cm / 16.5 × 16.5 cm

Dummy, 1997-2003
49 framed collages consisting
of post-its with handwritten
notes attached to dummy sheets
from Pia Arke's original dummy
for her book work *Stories from
Scoresbysund: Photographs,
Colonisation and Mapping*,
Borgen, 2003
Each (framed): 24.5 × 42 cm

Pia Arke and Anders Jørgensen
*Tupilakosaurus: An Interesting
Study about the Triassic Myth of
Kap Stosch*, 1999
Video 4:3 (S-VHS video to DVD)
Duration: 9:18 min

Sweden

Malmö Konstmuseum

*Untitled (Toying with National
Costume)*, c. 1993
Black-and-white contact sheet
20 × 15 cm
Inv.no. MMK 9841

*Untitled (Put Your Kamik on Your
Head so Everyone Can See Where
You Came From)*, c. 1993
Black-and-white contact sheet
20 × 15 cm
Inv.no. MMK 9840

Perlustration, 1994
Gelatin silver print on baryte
paper
37 × 43.3 cm
Inv.no. MMK 9839

*Pia Arke and Anders Jørgensen
Tupilakosaurus: An Interesting
Study about the Triassic Myth of
Kap Stosch*, 1999
Video 4:3 (S-VHS video til DVD)
Duration: 9:18 min
Inv.no. MMK 9844

Moderna Museet

Nature Morte alias
Perlustrations 1-10, 1994
10 silver gelatin prints on
baryte paper
Dimensions variable
Donated by the artist, 1996

The Kronborg Series alias *The
Kronborg Suite*, 1996
7 Silver gelatin prints on
baryte paper, pinhole camera
photographs
Each 50 × 60 cm
Donated by the artist, 1996

USA

**Collection Albright-Knox Art
Gallery, Buffalo, New York**

*Untitled (Pinhole Camera
Photograph with "Horse")*,
c. 1990-1995
Parchment paper, paint and hair
on pinhole camera negative
49 × 58.5 cm

*Untitled (Pinhole Camera
Photograph with "Teapot")*,
c. 1990-1995
Parchment paper, paint and hair
on silver gelatin baryte paper
48.8 × 59 cm

Arctic Hysteria, 1996
Video 4:3 (S-VHS video to DVD)
Duration: 5:55 min

The Explorers Club, New York

Nuugaarsuk alias *Pinhole Camera
Photograph* alias *The Point*, 1990
Gelatin silver print on baryte
paper
49.5 × 59.5 cm

Perlustration 6, 1994
Silver gelatin print on baryte
paper
Dimensions unknown

This list contains all works by Pia Arke in public collections that Louisiana Museum of Modern Art has been able to locate prior to this publication.

The catalogue is published on the occasion of the exhibition
Pia Arke
Dream and Repression
Louisiana Museum of Modern Art, Humlebæk
15 July 2021 - 2 January 2022

Kunsten Museum of Modern Art Aalborg
14 January - 18 April 2022

Kunstmuseum Brandts, Odense
12 May - 25 September 2022

Curator: Anders Kold
Curatorial Coordinator / Registrar: Marie Mose Hyllested
Exhibition Architect: Jens Kamp
Conservator/Exhibition Producer: Jesper Lund Madsen
Graphic Design: Marie d'Origny Lübecker
Exhibition Assistant: Helle Fagralid

The exhibition at the Louisiana Museum of Modern Art is supported by:

C.L. DAVIDS FOND OG SAMLING

The catalogue is supported by:

NY
CARLSBERG
FONDET

NEW CARLSBERG FOUNDATION

Photos: p. 8, 18-19, 72-73, 74, 91 above: Anders Sune Berg; p. 11: Kim Hansen; p. 12-13, 31, 38, 93-97, 107: Poul Buchard / Brøndum & Co.; p. 20, 58, 67, 82: Peter Baastrup; p. 24-25: Søren Arke; p. 27: courtesy of the artist and Metro Pictures, New York; p. 46: Mette Sandbye; p. 50-54, 64-65: Courtesy of Kunstmuseum Brandts; p. 86-87: Michael Petersen